Judy Ann MacMillan was born
1945. When she was seven years
invited her to paint with him ar
her life. She went on to train at
College of Art & Design in Dundee, Scotland and held her first show in Jamaica when she was twenty-two. She has been exhibiting both at home and abroad ever since. Best known for the finely observed portraits and the landscapes of her beloved homeland, her truthful observation, classical rendering and empathy for sitters have brought her international acclaim. In 2007, she was inducted into the Hall of Fame, by the Caribbean Foundation for the Arts for her outstanding contribution in the field of art. She lives in Jamaica, dividing her time between Kingston and her rural retreat, Rockfield, in the parish of St Ann.

Her first book, *My Jamaica: The Paintings of Judy Ann MacMillan,* was published in 2004.

BORN YA

The Life and Loves of a Jamaican Painter

Judy Ann MacMillan

My autobiography

Beattie Books

First published in Great Britain in 2019
by Beattie Books

3 5 7 9 10 8 6 4 2

A CIP catalogue record for this book is
available from the British Library.

ISBN (hardback) 978-1-5272-3523-6
ISBN (paperback) 978-1-5272-3745-2
Available as an ebook

Illustration opposite: 'Tools of the Trade' (Peta Gay MacMillan)

Designed and typeset by Helen Ewing
Set in Latin 725 BT

Printed & Bound in Great Britain by TJ International,
Padstow, Cornwall

www.beattiebooks.co.uk

To my mother, Vida, who gave me life and the courage to live it

Contents

Illustrations

Section One

Section Two

Inell Atkinson, dear friend, confidant and my interpreter of present day Jamaica (Peta Gay MacMillan)

Edward Lucie-Smith and me at the book launch of, *My Jamaica*. London, 2004 (Olivia McGilchrist)

With Jonathan Clark at the London Show, 2011

Publisher, Nick Gillard, at the London Show, 2011

Dave & Alexei, father & son

David Alexander Russell & Sabrina Cesolini at their wedding, Rockfield, 12 May 2001 (Peta Gay MacMillan)

My three granddaughters: Zoe; Francesca & Sofia (Alexei Russell)

Zoe & Francesca patiently wait while Mr Chisholm strips sugar cane for them (Alexei Russell)

Alexei's women, Christmas 2017 (Alexei Russell)

My family

Working on 'My Land', as I named the painting, with my favourite painting companion, beloved Rocky the Rottweiler (Kit von Zweigbergk)

'But I man on ya, I man born ya
I nah leave ya fi go America
No way sah, pot a boil ya, a belly full ya
Sweet Jamaica'

Pluto Shervington

Prologue

If yuh born fe hang, yuh cyan drown

The light wakes me. As my eyes open I feel that familiar quickening as I recognise that I'm in my favourite room in the world – my almost empty, white bedroom at Rockfield. Across from the bed are two pale rectangles of light, one a little askew and through these open windows drifts the cool, morning air.

'I like it here Mom, it feels pure.'

My son Alexei at five years old has honey-colored curls, streaked by the sun and his father's eyes. We are inseparable.

My painting is on the easel at the foot of the bed. It looks terrible in that first glance but I think I know what to do.

I go straight to the window although I can tell already that the light is going to be good today. Yes it's perfect.

A glorious panorama spreads before me, layers of hills from a height of sixteen hundred feet sloping down to the most tender dividing line of land and sea, a silent sea which is more air than water, turning imperceptibly into sky that reflects the water, its streaking clouds outlined in light. The smell of the wet oil paint from my canvas excites me. I grab the painting and head downstairs for coffee.

'I can't wait to paint! I can't wait to paint!'

I'm full of hope. Today is the day I'll get it right.

As I rush through the house turning off outside light switches, the wooden floor feels clean beneath my bare feet as yesterday on arrival I swept the whole place to lighten that musty smell of a locked-up house.

'If you want a clean house Judy Ann, clean it yourself and lock it behind you. Those people will leave filthy little bits of rag everywhere and redistribute the dirt with their unwashed mops. They will ruin all the appliances too and steal all the tools.'

Wait, yu hear dat? Who shi calling tief?

The kitchen windows are traditional batten windows without glass; when they are open they leave no division from the barbeques, the arched bamboos at the perimeter of the backyard and the ackee trees. The ackee trees are trimmed to repeat that arch but they keep exuberantly breaking out of formation.

When the windows were cut, the carpenter made one bigger than the other so the smaller one had to be adjusted to the larger size.

'But yu nevah seh dat yu want de two window de same size?'

'Yes, my mistake.'

These failures to anticipate or differences of opinion can be seen all over the house and many from way before I came here. Butt hinges have been put on splayed flat and taps turn in unexpected ways – the hot water is not always on the right.

On the kitchen counter there is always a still life of fruit and vegetables ready to eat or paint and every room has a bouquet of flowers or leaves from the garden with whatever is blooming. To bring the outdoors inside on arrival has become a habit, which starts the creative energy going, rather like priming a pump.

'But Mom, you can't paint *everything*?'

'That's what you think.'

The ratio of visual impulse to completed picture is about one to a thousand and what controls the selection of the image that gets painted is mysterious even to me.

My mornings are the foundation of the day. I savour each one in the vibrating air, loud with the eternal hum of insects, birds and hidden creatures. My much-washed painting clothes are so comfortable that I can forget them.

There's no one to stop me.

'I can't wait to paint!'

I stare at the painting with a critical gaze while drinking the coffee. When the light is perfect I begin.

It takes sometimes an hour to get a rhythm going. At first I am edgy and whisper a prayer to God to help me. Nothing is right as the new strokes break into the existing relationships but slowly the network of adjustments become rhythmic and automatic. I forget myself completely and someone deep inside me paints.

Coming up to 12.30, hunger brings me back to the surface. I take the painting inside, as I want to see it for the first time out of that light.

What's for lunch? Oh, whatever is there, maybe a sweet potato fresh from the earth and roasted in its skin with a green salad. Thank God, I don't have to leave the hilltop today to get drinking water, gas for the lawnmower, or anything at all in the choked tiny aisles of the nearest country supermarket. The chores can wait. If the roof falls in I'm going to paint all day.

Nowadays, by three o'clock my energy slips a little. In Kingston I must lie down for an hour. In the country, where it is cool, I can go awhile longer, maybe preparing for the next day. I may ground a canvas, glaze another painting that is dry enough, or block in a still life so that I can work on the days when I'm too tired to face the outdoor sun. I wash my brushes and stop for the day.

It feels good to get the sodden painting clothes off and shed the strong smell of turpentine. To 'tidy for the afternoon' is a habit that comes from childhood. Its purpose was to be ready for visitors but those days are long gone. At four o'clock you would sit on the verandah and friends would drop in without notice. Now I don't even bother to open the gate. After an intense day of painting, I feel as drained as a cup inverted on its saucer and there is a type of conversation that makes me even more tired.

'Suh, what yu do when you're up here by yusself?'

'Paint.'

'Jus paint? Yu don't get bored?'

I do find the evenings lonely. I put a load of laundry in the washing machine, walk listlessly around the garden, never ceasing to be amazed at the beauty of the sky and the arms of the enormous valley holding the sea. The fragility of this soap bubble, this reverie, that is my home.

I look at the morning's work in the artificial light of the studio until I can't look at the painting anymore.

I enjoy how the house looks lit in the evening and may have a drink on the verandah, a toast to the main attraction, the sunset: admiring again the elegant contours of the dark palm trees against a rich sky.

The phone startles me – still a pleasure after fifteen years without one – and an American accent lifts my heart.

'Judy, I was just saying to Chris, I hope she's not sitting on that verandah by herself!'

'That's exactly what I'm doing. Yes, it's beautiful down here, how is it up there?'

Ever notice how the choices that we make earlier turn into traps? Well, just ask me.

Suddenly a sweet voice brings me out of my daydream and back to the present, 'Nonna, Nonna Nonna!'

A sturdy little body with a round face, full of joy, is running up the steps towards me. Another, more serious, little one is following like a shadow. The baby behind them is unsteadily trying to keep up.

It's my granddaughters, Francesca, Zoe and Sofia and they are racing into my outstretched arms, just as Alexei used to years ago.

1

School Days and West Avenue

Rock stone ah river bottom nuh know sun hot

If you spend your whole life in a very small place it's like living in a parable. It is impossible to miss the meaning of life with one's nose pressed into it at such close range. When you never lose sight of the people you were at kindergarten with and as those familiar faces age before you at each year's Christmas parties, it is possible to know the beginning, middle and end of every story.

This closeness creates a claustrophobia that can be oppressive. Traveling daily through the monotonous labyrinth of the same shabby streets can feel like a prison. At these times the surrounding sea feels like a wall that is standing up and the sky feels like a lid. The heat inside the overcrowded cell is suffocating.

I would leave Jamaica and my leaving felt like escape but invariably I would need that human contact again and long for family life and identity. The navel string would tug, the yearning grow and I would rush back from those refreshingly wide and impersonal landscapes to the humid island incubator that was my home.

They say that you are not a Jamaican unless you have stood barefoot under a mango tree stoning and eating them while they are still warm from the sun. I will go further and say you are not a Jamaican unless you can aim that stone to hit the stem exactly where the fruit joins the branch and catch it before it falls to the ground.

In my earliest memories I am standing barefoot with my brother under a Bombay mango tree in the backyard at West Avenue. I am looking up at that magnificent umbrella of leaves against the blue sky – an intricate pattern of flickering light and shade – to see the ripe ones. I bite mine right there, the sweetness makes my head swim and the juice runs down my face and arms.

West Avenue in Constant Spring was my home from 1945, the year of my birth, until I left to get married at the age of twenty-two. It is also the home of memory and of those dreams that slip away too quickly on waking.

It was years later when studying art history that I realised the house was a perfect example of the Art Deco style. It caused much consternation as it was being built and my father was able to buy two adjoining lots cheaply because the owners did not want to build beside 'a madman'. With the resulting extra land, it sat way back from the road on three acres.

Oh suh, madness is in de *family*

The garden had been planted by my grandmother and contained every type of fruit tree imaginable. Aside from mangoes (both Julie and Bombay) there were cocoa plums as well as sweet sops and sour sops. There were huge tamarind trees one of which had a slatted wooden bench around the trunk and there was a chair on ropes so that we children could swing. There was a pond with bullfrogs, fish and the odd water lily. There was also an extraordinary canon ball tree in the middle of the front lawn. Strange waxy flowers with a sickly smell grew right out of its truck and it became the subject of one of my first paintings.

'That damn tree makes such a mess. One day I'm going to chop it down.'

A row of tall acacias shaded the driveway and under them grew gigantic ferns. On the lower branches of a lignum vitae tree, with wood as dense as stone, hung orchids in clay pots. In 1951 this tree was severed, as though with a machete by Hurricane Charlie, leaving a stump which remained there in memoriam to the event. That same night my brother and I watched goggle-eyed, as the lawn in front of our house became a river.

Gilbert? No sah, dat was nutting to Charlie. Charlie man, every roof blow wey!

The best thing may have been a folly: brick steps with an arch under the steps designed to look like the entrance to an old Great House. It was covered in a coarse vine that we called 'ivy'.

'What used to be there?'

'I built it', my father would say, 'I love ruins and I didn't have one so I built one.'

Lawd have mercy, that Dudley MacMillan is really something …

The big back yard was an enchanted world and my brother and I would play endless games. Davy Crockett was a favourite: we took turns to play the part inventing a friend for him called 'Pal' so that we could always both take part. Far from our mother's eyes, we learnt from the gardener how to roast a sweet potato on a little fire and lit thin brown sticks, which we elaborately puffed pretending they were cigarettes. We learnt to climb trees and when my bookworm phase replaced my tomboy phase I would read up in their branches. Later we had a couple of cows that ate my *Learning to Draw* book left forgotten in a big pile of grass where I was reading. I mourned the loss of this fascinating book which showed how to join up two circles and make a horse and how to repeat the length of the head seven times to get the correct length of the body. After the cows, we had a pony called Dandy but I hated riding and fell off crippling my left hand and rapidly lost all interest in horses after that.

At the back was a little wooden house raised off the ground where the maids and a gardener lived. It amused them when I sneaked round there to sample the delicious food we were not allowed to eat from their pots.

'Oh my God, all that starch!'

The neighbourhood that surrounded West Avenue consisted of four avenues in a rectangle, lined with deeply lawned houses set far back from the road. They had open verandahs with ferns in clay pots on pedestals. It was quiet. You could hear the birds and sometimes in the early morning the clip clop hooves of the donkey that pulled the bread cart which occasionally I was allowed to ride, sitting up beside the driver who shouted, 'Bull-ah. Sugah-bun. Cocoa-bread!'

Apart from that and the singing calls of the peanut man with his whistle it was as quiet as the countryside.

Inside the house was cool with Cuban-tiled floors or wooden floors slippery smooth under our bare feet: they were polished every morning and mopped every afternoon. Most importantly the walls were covered in murals: two geese flew on a curved grey wall in the living-room; a pair of life size children lay on a beach in my parent's bathroom; an exquisite line drawing of Pan playing his pipes was on the verandah and there were waist high birds all around the walls of the guest room. These were painted by Carl Abrahams. There was also a big Rhoda Jackson in the dining room and a wonderful Albert Huie bought from his first show.

In the bookcase there was a large leather-bound book that looked like a Bible called 'World Famous Masterpieces'.

'If you want to look at that book, Judy Ann, make sure your

hands are clean. Be very careful turning the pages because that is a very precious book.'

I approached it with awe and that is where I first met Leonardo da Vinci, Gainsborough, Watteau, Botticelli, Constable, Vermeer and Turner. For every birthday and every Christmas I received from my father, my favourite thing, a new art book. Confined to bed with chicken pox, I spent the hours trying not to scratch with Rembrandt. The first drawing of children is often a house with a door, two windows and the sun with rays above. I remember joining several of these together.

'What are you drawing Judy Ann?'

'Hotels.'

By the age of four I was already a dead serious artist. There is a letter written to my parents around this time. They were in New York and my letter asks whether they have shown the people they were staying with my war picture yet as they had promised. There is another letter from my father saying that he is coming home and bringing 'a paint set for Judy and a ball for Robert'.

I met Albert Huie when I was about seven years old. He lived very close to our house and my father stopped one day to give him a lift. As he entered the car, he was holding a canvas turned face in and I asked to see the painting. When he turned it round I gasped, 'You must be a genius!'

My father laughed with delight at my reaction and took me to visit his studio. That studio was thrilling to me. The smell of the oil paint was delicious. I had only used gouache and powder paint on paper at school but here there were huge juicy gobs of paint and what looked like a hundred brushes. The organised chaos and the layers of paintings in progress were like visual electricity to my childish eyes.

Albert, who never patronised children, saw the spark of interest and invited me to come painting with him. I was too shy to speak very much but we went up to Gordon Town to one of his habitual painting spots. I don't remember what I did as I was probably too overwhelmed to do very much.

Carl Abrahams came to the house and gave me a few lessons in drawing when I was about eight years old. He discouraged my imaginative pictures inspired by comics and illustrations and encouraged me to paint local subject matter.

At Wolmer's High School for Girls, the art teacher was an amazing character called Miss Edna DaCosta. She had a round face absolutely plastered in powder of a most unrealistic shade of salmon pink, like that Flesh tint that comes in tubes. Her slit of a mouth was painted dark crimson, like Clara Bow, over another plainly discernible mouth of a different shape. This on top of a slab of body and a voice that boomed whenever she spotted me, 'Judy MacMillan … GET into the art room!'

Occasionally, I would whimper, 'Ahmmmm but I'm supposed to be at History class.'

'NONSENSE. I'll speak to the history teacher!'

One day Albert Huie telephoned the house and asked to speak to me.

'Did you really like that painting that you admired in my studio?'

'Oh yes,' I squeaked.

'Well I finished it and you can have it for twelve pounds.'

My father gave me the money and I bought it. It was of a girl putting a hibiscus in her hair. I treasure it still for many reasons. First for the compliment that he paid to my childish appreciation and later, when I became a working artist, for the glimpse that story gives into the everyday hustle of the artist who must make a sale to live because it is his only income. It was the first of many lessons he was to teach me by example.

My first oil painting was done on a school outing with Mrs Josephs, another art teacher from Wolmer's. It was of an avenue of acacia trees at Hope Gardens. I adored doing it and still have it. The experience was marred for me by my teacher putting in the shadows across the road. She made them very blue and I did not see them quite that blue.

My first sale was when I was eleven and took place at Hills Gallery on Harbour Street, which was Kingston's only gallery and art supply store (founded by Christopher and Norah Hills). The manager was an exotic Chinese woman called Iris Day who made an important contribution to the cultural life of Kingston. I encountered many artists there. Daniel Heartman's highly rendered pencil portraits of Rasta's impressed me greatly as did Eric Smith's garden paintings. While Susan Alexander's market scenes, with a repeated note of colour playing across the canvas, opened my eyes to new harmonies.

A small exhibition was put on of precocious students' work and a gouache of mine was hung high up on the wall. I had developed a technique of loading the brush with yellow or red paint and flicking it so that the paint would splatter across the picture and give an enormous amount of atmosphere to my carnival scene. To my intense excitement a red sticker went up on my picture.

'Who bought my painting?' I asked the boy on the ladder.

'MacMillan.'

'No, that's my name. What's the name of the person who bought it?'

'MacMillan.'

It was my father.

'Daddy, how could you? You made a fool of me.'

'But darling, I thought you would be pleased.'

I still have the card that says, 'With compliments of Hills Galleries. Two pounds and ten shillings.'

Although I left High School a virtual ignoramus, as I spent my school days entirely in the art room, I won some awards. The best prize was a trip to Miami with my art teacher. I had never been abroad and a little red suit with white piping and box-pleated skirt was made for me to wear. My whole family, cousins and aunts, came to the airport to wave us off. My parents came but also Val Bloomfield, a young Scottish girl, newly out of art school in Glasgow. She had come to teach at Wolmer's after marrying a Jamaican. She was going through extreme culture shock not helped in any way by the reigning Miss DaCosta.

I don't believe there was any art gallery in Miami at the time. My viewing began from inside the plane because through the window when we landed I saw on the tarmac blonde young men who looked like the stars I worshipped at the matinee working like labourers. I had never seen that before. How different was the world outside my cradle.

After the week in Miami, at a hotel on Flagler Street, my parents took me on to New York. We stayed on Charles Street in 'The Village' and to my absolute delight my father became my guide to the city, picking from that vast menu what he knew would stimulate me most. Not so much the Rockettes at Radio City Music Hall, as three unforgettable nights at a Jazz Festival on Randall's Island where I heard among others the great Gene Krupa. We went to Birdland where I got Miles Davis's autograph but most importantly we went to The Museum of Modern Art.

For the first time I saw, in the original, the paintings that I had seen in my books. I still remember and always will the effect those paintings had on me. *The Starry Night* by Vincent van Gogh made my knees give way and I had to sit down. The only other thing that could do that to me were the men that I was instantly and intensely attracted to. That was still to come. The point being that the powerful effect of these paintings was *physical. The Sleeping Gypsy* by Henri Rousseau washed me in goose bumps, as did *Guernica* by Pablo Picasso. A life-size Rodin lay on the floor of a small gallery and was the only object in the room while his *Burghers of Calais* was situated outside in the sculpture garden. I was fifteen years old and without any doubt I was going to art school.

My friends in my school days were Mary Hanna and Richild Springer. I met both at Wolmer's Prep School. I was allowed to go to their houses to spend the day and even allowed sometimes to spend the night. The two households provided a great contrast and is one of the greatest assets of a Jamaican upbringing. Mary came from one of the richest families in Kingston. Her father, a Lebanese merchant, had built an empire, which employed three thousand people. He was a great philanthropist in the colonial style in that he gave without fanfare. A wing of a hospital would be donated with only a small plaque unobtrusively placed to commemorate the gift.

Mrs Hanna was my example of a great society lady. She was always exquisitely groomed and the wonderful scent of 'White Shoulders' perfume wafted around her as, dressed in a Schiaparelli gown, she would descend the curving staircase into the ballroom at their mansion, Knole.

Looking like a tiny Grace Kelly, every afternoon she would sit on her verandah with its spectacular view of Kingston. With banks of orchids and hibiscus all around her, tea would be served on English china to an ever changing but ever present court. On Saturday afternoons their chauffeur would collect Mary, her younger brother Charles, my brother Robert and me and we would all go the movies at various cinemas in Kingston.

Although we knew they were rich we would certainly not have described them this way back then. They were just our friends and the delights that we took in their grand house, with its swimming pool and tennis court, were equated in our estimation with getting dirty in the backyard, climbing trees and all sorts of innocent broken taboos at ours.

By contrast, Richild's house was a spare white clapboard house on the grounds of the University. Her father was the archetype of a true intellectual. He had been educated at Oxford University and spoke eight languages.

'Including Greek, my dear.'

With his friend and neighbour Phillip Sherlock, they founded the University of The West Indies and became its first Chancellors. They were both knighted for their work.

Richild's mother was also beautiful with two white streaks in her jet-black hair like wings. There were some paintings at their house that I have never forgotten. In particular a Hector Whistler water colour of a black man's face that I loved. Mrs Springer liked to look after children for family and friends so the house was like a crèche and every afternoon all these babies would be bathed and dressed with shoes and socks put on and heads of hair combed to choruses in that Barbadian accent, 'Oooooh, who is so sweet. My, my, my, who is so sharp!'

When we dressed to go to the movies Mary and I would wear a little pale pink lipstick and crinolines but Richild would oil her skin, arms and legs and that was her only cosmetic. Mary was white and Richild was black.

She bringing colour into it now

Come with me to one of the all-day Sunday parties of my childhood.

They are already dancing as they come out of their cars. The women are glamorous in high-heeled sandals and clothes that show their bodies. They are every shade of brown. The men sway in sports shirts to a live calypso band. Many of them have little clipped moustaches and crinkly hair cut short. They smell of 'Limacol' or 'Bay Rum' splashes.

'Come and give Uncle Junior a kiss, sweet heart. What a way you're growing. Big girl now.'

An enormous group of maids in starched white uniforms and little caps keep their eyes on the children who are playing in the pool all day getting sunburned. Gardeners double as barmen and parking attendants for the day.

'You know my drink, eh Winston? Gin and tonic, put a little bitters.'

They drink rum and ginger, rum and coconut water, rum and coke with lots of ice. They drink gin and tonic, whisky and soda, vodka less frequently, with handfuls of salted peanuts or hard white crackers, piled high with solomon gundy or 'pick-up' saltfish.

At around three o'clock, a huge buffet lunch is put on the table. The meal is heavy with roasted legs of pork as well as chicken, beef and fish. There is always rice and red kidney beans cooked in coconut milk, plantains sliced and fried, bowls of mango chutney and scotch bonnet peppers put whole on the table with a little knife to cut them.

The dancing gets more lascivious after lunch. The men press their groins against the women. The laughter gets louder. The musicians grin.

Where did the naughty likkle flea go?
Nobaddy know, nobaddy know …'
All de boys love Mary Ann
Why do de boys love Mary Ann?

Cause she can BURRRRRUPPPPS like no one can
That's why de boys love Mary Ann

'Get out of the pool this minute you have had much too much sun. No, you can't stay for "Murder-in-the-dark". It's time to go home. Say "Thank you, Mrs Rose for a lovely day". In the car, in the car, in the car ... Dudley ... I don't believe you are having another drink ... you were the one who said you were ready to leave!'

'Just one for the road man ... tek it easy, tek it easy. Soon come.'

Years later I realised that, although we thought we were English, the culture was really closer to Latin America. I felt at home in Mexico and Peru and as though I had been born in Rio when I saw the people sitting in the sidewalk cafes laughing and jeering at each other for hours. Their humour was rooted in self-mockery just like ours. The only difference was language.

2

Daddy

Massa hawse, massa grass

Like a great many little girls, I was in love with my father but in the divided territory of my parent's marriage I was steadfastly on my mother's side.

Sometimes when I was three or four, he would come to my bedside before dawn and take me for a drive into the hills behind Kingston to bush land (now covered with huge mansions) to pick guavas, mangos or plums. Still dressed in the clothes from his nightclub he would be humming under his breath, 'C'est si bon.'

Sometimes he pulled the car over on the way to school, after my tearful confession that I hadn't done the homework that I had already lied to my mother about doing, allowing me to frantically scribble in my exercise book. I adored him at those times with a heart-bursting love that filled my universe. I still stop at a coconut cart almost daily to drink a water coconut and scoop out the jelly just as he used to. I still think about him every day.

He was a poor boy who grew up in a tiny wooden house in Rae Town in Kingston. I know so little about his parents but from one of the few photographs I have there is an image of a little jalousie windowed wooden house and standing in front of it a morose looking, dark man who was his father.

Hear dat? an shi tink shi white yu know

There is also a pale white woman, with a sad oval face, who was his mother. My father loved his mother but never spoke much about the disappointing man who was his own father. Any mysterious gaps in the family story – the whispers or sudden silences when we children entered the room were usually caused by shame. There was some unexplained fall from standards of respectability: alcoholism perhaps; 'he drank you know'; or some sexual indiscretion described in those days as 'taking advantage' of women.

This grandfather of mine, who I was recently fascinated to learn had worked as a timekeeper on the Panama Canal where my father had been born in 1909, is still shrouded in mystery. Whatever the behavior that had caused my grandmother to flee from him, she arrived with her infant sons in Jamaica around 1909. According to her two tight-lipped and disapproving sons, my father Dudley and his brother Egerton, she provided for them by sewing gentlemen's shirts with precious little help from the man of the family.

'Read this,' my father said one day, when I was in my twenties, shoving a clipped newspaper article towards me that he had clearly related to strongly, 'My childhood was like this.'

I read with widening eyes about this hard life in a tiny house with a bamboo gutter leading rainwater off the roof into a barrel. He was a self-made man and I marveled that he had come so far and catapulted us along with him. This achievement should have taken a couple of generations at least, however by the age of twenty-five he had built that house where we grew up. Yet his story is not untypical of an island that from its start was associated with getting rich quickly.

In those more modest days to be poor was not an indictment. The greatest people in Jamaica, Sir Phillip Sherlock for example, was the son of a Baptist minister and grew up too poor to afford to go to school. Yet by the time he did get to his first school aged ten he had read the whole of Dickens.

My father won one of the first scholarships given for education to Wolmer's Boys School – still one of the best schools on the island. His early scars were caused by the social ostracism of the times directed to anyone who did not pay for their education. The cruelest form that this took was to be denied the privilege of playing sports. From the many times he mentioned this I could tell the depth of that early wound. However, self-pity is not a characteristic of that Second World War generation and he focused on academics, excelling at English, becoming the editor of the school magazine. Proud of his early successes he often told the story of how an English teacher, to show appreciation for one of his essays, gave him a grade of 'one hundred and TEN out of a hundred!'

His charismatic charm came from a complete lack of bitterness, the ability to reinvent his life continuously and also to find the humour in just about everything, starting with himself.

'I'm born brand new every morning,' he would say as he sliced into a rare steak with tomatoes at the breakfast table. Or, 'I don't need to go to church', when my mother was herding us into the car on Sundays, 'I am on a hot-line to God!'.

Lawd, Mr Mac was a lovely man but de wife did facety bad

Powerfully driven to escape poverty, most likely in reaction to the problem father who had caused his mother such enormous pain, within a week of leaving High School he started work as a messenger boy at the local newspaper, *The Daily Gleaner*.

'Let me tell you something, the best thing you can do for the poor is not be one of them!'

A friend, who in later years became Editor of the newspaper, had been interviewed for the same job that day and they had both been hired. However, Daddy got five shillings a week more than Theodore Sealy's ten shillings making his salary a whopping fifteen shillings a week. He said it was because his skin was 'a lighter shade of brown than Sealy's'.

Fyah! Powah! All dat foolnish-nis soon stap when Black Man Time come

They laughed at this injustice over whisky and soda all their lives. Meanwhile, my father's good looks and personality brought him to the attention of a group of rich businessmen who put together the money to get him some exposure to the outside world – a practice that still exists today for promising youths. This allowed him to go to The World's Fair in New York in 1939. While in New York he was invited to his first Manhattan cocktail party. Everyone was standing up but one woman, conspicuously, was lying down on a sofa. As he approached her she said, 'Lie down. I hear that you are a good conversationalist.' Her name was Judy and the family story is that I was named after this unconventional woman.

My father started the first advertising agency in Jamaica. How it came about became another much told family story of a man who, while struggling to succeed, always made things look as though they were charmed.

He was standing looking at the construction of a big new state of the art department store that was being built on King Street, the main shopping street of the town. The owner, Abe Issa, came down the street and stopped for a chat. My father suggested that he should advertise the opening of the store and drew an ad on a paper bag he was carrying to demonstrate. He was immediately hired and so 'The House of Issa' became the biggest account of Jamaica's first ever advertising agency.

Another revealing story about being interviewed for another account was of him sitting quietly listening to a prominent mogul of the time giving an extended monologue. The big man finally said, 'You know you are a very puzzling young man'.

'How so?'

'Well, you want to work for me but you have been here for twenty minutes and haven't given me one idea that could improve my business.'

'I wasn't aware that I'd been given the job yet.'

Advertising was always his main line of work but the entertainment business was his true passion. He started off putting on musical reviews in the vaudeville format with names like 'Hot Chocolate'. He followed this up with 'variety acts' that he booked for The Colony Club, a new nightclub that he built in Cross Roads. This comprised an open-aired terrace with a coconut tree in the middle, a covered stage, dance floor and a large square bar. Along the top of the wall in the bar was a spectacular bas-relief frieze in concrete, which had been sculpted by the prominent artist, Alvin Marriot. It depicted stylised frogs, lizards, tropical leaves and figures displayed in the elegant Deco style that was so fashionable at the time. It was much loved so when my father tore down the night club to build a cinema on the same location the bar was saved and, like the nucleus of a changing cell, that room would become my gallery many years later.

Every one who was anyone danced at The Colony Club including the Governor's wife, Lady Molly Huggins. She pioneered a new model for all English Governor's wives with her philanthropic involvement and shaping of Jamaican society. I was allowed to go to the club at night only once dressed in white organdy to see a comic artist whose act involved drawing lightning fast cartoons on a big drawing pad. But occasionally, usually due to some domestic emergency, my brother and I would have to sleep in the car in our pajamas, clutching pillows and going to sleep to the sound of the band inside. We would be awakened by their laughter, my mothers perfume and my father's voice, 'Little troupers, little troupers!'

This was inevitably followed by their quarrel on the way home.

A series of entertainers passed through our lives. There were strippers from Havana, singers from America, dancers, magicians and trapeze artists from Europe who stayed in our guest room. The women were glamorous; when they opened their luggage the clothes inside felt cold and smelled of perfume and cigarette smoke as they shook out the wrinkles and hung them up. They would lie naked to sunbathe on the flat roof of the verandah where I would be sent with lemonade for them. They would sign glossy black and white studio publicity photographs, 'To Darling Dudley and Vida'. Our family albums filled up with them.

There was the story of one stripper who was scheduled and advertised to perform on the narrow stage of a cinema in Cross Roads. Just before the show the police arrived and announced that she could not perform because the venue was a public one, not a private club, for which different laws applied. My father thought for a minute while the 'artiste' hovered nervously and the audience had started to arrive.

'Go on stage naked and get dressed!', he told her. There was no law against that and reveals the street-smart thinking of the born entrepreneur.

The club collapsed under the weight of signed credit cards that could not be collected but the cinema was already squeezing out that nightclub era. So he built his own cinema on the site of the nightclub. This cinema, which could seat just over two thousand people, was a fully equipped small theatre as well, complete with dressing rooms, an orchestra pit and a deep stage. He became an impresario, presenting concerts by the simple means of persuading the managers of orchestras and musicians to make Kingston either the first stop, or the last, on their South American tours. The best music in the world – The Berlin Philharmonic, The London Philharmonic, Yehudi Menuhin, and Albert Ferber – all played in Kingston because of him.

For the less cultivated, he also presented famous pop stars like Bill Haley and the Comets and Nat King Cole. He had outstripped the strippers from Havana. Usually the classical concerts made just enough money to pay the musicians but he continued to offer them as a contribution to the place where he had prospered.

I spent a great deal of my childhood at these cinemas of Kingston as we had free passes to all of them and when the double bill, two for the price of one came in, it was not uncommon to see six films in one day. He started a Film Society that showed award-winning films like, *The Bicycle Thief* and *Rashomon* for the small and ever dwindling crowd who sought quality. Until the day there was no audience at all.

A popular satirical show called 'Eight O'clock Jamaica Time' referred to him directly, 'I called the State Theatre the other day and the manager, Mr MacMillan himself answered the phone.'

'What's on?' I asked.

'We are showing a World War One movie with the original cast.'

'What time does it begin?'

'What time can you make it?'

This creative milieu of moneymaking schemes and dreams;

the ice tinkling in the glasses of whisky and soda, the cigarette smoke, the deals with foreign fly-by-night charlatans, carpet-bagging through the tropics outsmarting the local boys, was my fathers world. The continuous parties at our house for celebrities and the enormous fun that he found in all of it, is an aura that surrounds all memories of my father.

3

Mummy

Shi likkle but shi tallawah

She was the movie star of my childhood and I thought her the most beautiful woman in the world. I would lie on her bed and watch the evening ritual, which involved covering her face with layers of cold cream and closing her pores with witch hazel. She was small and curvy with red hair, a turned up nose and green eyes exactly the colour of mine. I knew always that she adored me and I certainly loved her but I was terrified of her anger and that fear of displeasing her was constant.

Her background was quite different to my father because she was born in a small property in St Ann called, New Home. All Jamaicans know what that means.

Yes … shi face-ty

St Ann is known as 'The Garden Parish' because of its visual beauty. In my schooldays we would go there in the summer holidays and stay in modest little rented houses by the sea. But this was not the area that my mother called home. She was from the interior and spoke of a zinc bath pan being placed outside so it would fill with night dew for her father's icy bath in the morning. My mother was typical of people born in this part of Jamaica. She truly believed that it was the centre of the universe. They felt superior and entitled to look down on anyone who was not from there. They never forgot a slight; held on to grudges until death and found the very mildew of St Ann to be sacrosanct. As she herself put it, 'Vida Juanita Rose Fullerton doesn't suffer fools gladly.'

These attitudes help to explain why so many of the islands modern heroes, like Marcus Garvey and Bob Marley came from this area with its retentions in the collective cellular memory of the past. Memories of plantocracy at the top complete with delusions of grandeur while at the bottom a righteous justification for sabotage and a hunger for justice. Both the top and the bottom though shared equally resistance to change and would unite in an instant against the common enemy – *outsiders*.

Born on 3 June 1919, Vida was the eldest of a family of five: four girls and a boy. Her mainly absentee father was Sydney Leopold Fullerton who came from Brown's Town, St Ann. He worked most of his adult life as an accountant in Venezuela. Her mother was Hilda Ann Garcia, a telegraph clerk, who went from district to district sending and receiving messages. Hilda was so good at this that she eventually became the postmistress in Brown's Town.

Sydney and Hilda started off life in Ewarton, St Ann. In 1913, Sydney went to Cuba to seek his fortune, taking with him his young wife and their first two children – my mother Vida and her sister Hulia Alecia. My aunt Hulia nearly died there of a mysterious ailment and her gravesite was actually chosen by my distressed grandmother who was already pregnant with her third daughter, Peggy. Luckily, the baby's life was saved. The neighbours fed her paw paw to soothe the stomach, suggesting that the ailment was a digestive one.

The family returned to Jamaica when Sydney had earned enough money to buy a property in Alexandria, St Ann. An old house on the property was renovated and the name New Home stuck. And it was there that my mother's memories began.

She became the surrogate male of the family protecting her gentle mother from bill collectors and the humiliations of late school fees. For this role she developed a sharp tongue and a manner as imperious as Catherine of Russia.

'New Home' seems to have been lost quite early on in a way that remains unclear. The details are a rich blend of rural superstition. Details remain sketchy but they involve the ordered removal of a grave, a court case with a malevolent headman and a Duppy's revenge. Resistance to change continues even after death in St Ann. Whatever the truth of it all, my grandfather lost 'New Home' and he moved the family to Kingston where two more children were born, Maurice and Dorothy. He tried the grocery business with premises on East Queen Street, downtown Kingston, across the road from the upscale Myrtle Bank Hotel. In spite of this elegant location, the business failed. It was enough to make him believe in curses in an age when curses were taken seriously.

Donkey seh dis world no level, hill and gully yah so, hill a gully deh so

Sydney returned to South America where he had better luck and after a stint in Honduras settled as the accountant for an oil company in Venezuela. It was at this time my mother developed her role as family champion with a sarcastic tongue.

After many years successfully sending money home to support his family, Sydney discovered some financial chicanery and unwisely reported it to the powers that be. It was a case of killing the messenger and he was duly fired and returned to Jamaica for the last time – an embittered man.

Aiyee sah, dis life too hard. Yu suck salt troo a wooden spoon

The children of my mother's generation spent holidays in St Ann at the various country houses that belonged to their aunts. One of these, Windsor, is now a school. Another is Loch

Eric of which only the two gateposts remain. The family stories about these aunts often ended with, 'Oh poor Aunt Ethlind, she died of a broken heart, you know,' suggesting that while they lived there was no escape from the heartbreaking infidelities of their brutish, rural husbands. Every family has its secrets and in those days of children being seen but not heard (and certainly not joining in adult conversation) we would often catch the pursed lips or the sudden dropped voices and significant nods in our direction, 'Careful. The Children.'

The secrets were never told until the people involved were dead and sometimes dead for many years. This was not just in deference to their feelings but also because of a genuine fear of stirring up the wrath of powerful duppies.

'But why can't I call the names now that they are all quite dead?'

'Well, we don't know what happens after death Judy, so we should exercise some caution in letting out these secrets. Remember what happened to Grandpa.'

Not everything good fe hear, good fe talk

My mother's childhood was happy and she grew into a popular girl with a great figure who loved dancing, especially in polka dotted dresses with sweetheart necklines.

After her education at Wolmer's High School for Girls, she took a secretarial course and worked in the legal offices of Livingston, Alexander & Levy on Duke Street in Kingston. With her first pay cheque she bought a mahogany dressing table for her mother.

She was also engaged to be married 'with a diamond ring on my finger' when she first met my father. By then Dudley was one of Kingston's eligible bachelors and moving in an older, more sophisticated crowd. He was about to start up a political party with Abe Issa when they hired my mother to be their secretary. The political party never happened but my parents were married within three months, much to the dismay of both sides of the family. My father's friends were skeptical as my mother was an unknown ingénue. His mother was horrified and apparently ran screaming down their very long driveway in despair. Her parents, for whom he failed to meet any of the St Ann criteria, were also grieved and did not trust him an inch. And of course there was the poor fiancée who at least got back his diamond ring. At the wedding there was only a small group of immediate family with Abe Issa as the best man.

Lawd have mercy, what a sumting-ah hear Mas Dudley madda cry blood ovah it

My favourite photograph of them together shows a glamorous smiling couple: my father smiles below a clipped moustache, his white linen jacket a background for my mother's sweet, slightly mischievous face. They look exactly like the 1940's movie stars of the era but, significantly, they are also looking in different directions.

They were the most mismatched couple in a world of mismatched couples. My mother's only dream was to be a wife and mother. She should have had a man who came home after work and spent Sundays going to visit dear Aunt Maud or poor Aunt Ethlind. Instead, she got a workaholic who went to his nightclub after the advertising agency closed and, after the club closed, only came home to change clothes and get a little shut eye before going back to his advertsing agency.

She complained bitterly and with increasing vehemence to his muttered response, 'Try a little tenderness.'

Their battles were continuous with only temporary ceasefires for parties, trips and those times when my mother's loyalty and support were required. And she was loyal to the death – always fiercely on his side against his enemies long after he himself had already forgiven them. All friends of the family had to take a side, nothing was hidden and the whole melodrama was played out in front of us on a daily basis.

'Get in the car!', my father would bark.

'Children, get out of the car!', my mother would order.

Their battles were hilarious to most people but not to me. My mother's tears caused me huge distress. Worse than that, they made me terrified of marriage.

Every time the word 'divorce' was spoken we implored them to try again. My little sister, Peta Gay, eleven years younger than me, was supposed to save the marriage.

I still remember the first time I saw her and the joy of bringing her home, rocking her to sleep and feeding her. She became the adored 'baby' of the family and my mother's comfort and companion when I left for art school in Scotland.

The day Jamaica declared independence my mother wept all night. As far as she was concerned it was the end of the island and she was inconsolable. England and 'God Save the Queen' meant more to her than tea at four and roast beef for Sunday lunch. It meant: education; discipline; good manners; order; art; history; music; the rule of law and civilisation itself.

Two stories, which have acquired the status of legend in our family, show what life with this volatile mother was like. Stopped by a policeman and asked to spell her name my mother yelled, 'M-A-C-M-I-L-L-A-N!' and drove off at eighty miles an hour. The poor man gave chase on his motorcycle, which was no match for her Buick. My brother and I were pressed down flat to the floor during a tyre-screeching car chase through the streets of Kingston that was worthy of any Hollywood movie. In the end she pulled into a dark driveway and we watched him shoot past.

She would blow the horn loudly if I was not standing under

the designated tree to be collected from school. On one occasion the whole class was being kept in. Frozen with horror I sat at my desk and heard the horn, which meant that she was not only there but annoyed to be kept waiting. Worse, she appeared at the door of the classroom.

'Judy Ann, get in the car.'

'The whole class is being punished Mrs MacMillan,' explained the teacher.

'Oh? You are not, however, going to punish ME. Judy Ann get in the car immediately.'

Who shi tink she is? What a woman facety man!

She was no match for a higgler on the street however.

'My dear woman, ten pounds for a head of lettuce? You must be completely mad!'

'Eat de money den nuh,' was the higgler's laconic suggestion.

One day a street boy, one of the numerous loiterers who clustered outside the small Chinese groceries, said something impertinent to her as she passed by. Bolt upright, with her nose in the air, she looked up at him and asked, 'Why can't you ignore me as I ignore you?'

'Because ah love you,' he said with a wicked grin.

She went in and bought him a beer.

Her worst fears were realised When Michael Manley came to power and created, within two years, an exodus of the middle classes from Jamaica. She said she would burn her house to the ground and take to the hills with a rifle rather than be run out of her country. I was much too timid to shoot a rifle but I resolved to join her and make soup and roll bandages if it came to actual civil war.

Duppy know who fe frighten

My friends still talk about the day of the largest protest

march in opposition to Michael Manley in September 1979. It was to protest the arrival of the Cuban Ambassador, Ulises Estrada. In the '50s we had put up people fleeing from Cuba, as had so many Jamaicans. They passed through the island in droves. Propaganda was no match for the eyewitness accounts; we remembered their empty hands.

'Mummy, they are going to march.'

'Oh thank God, Judy Ann, come for me come for me. Come for me, NOW!'

Before I lost sight of her in the crowd that day, I glimpsed her shouting away at the helicopter circling above to control us dangerous reactionaries.

Dressed in a little cotton knitted number, jewelry and high heels (I don't think she could even walk in flat shoes) and ever mindful of her skin, a straw hat and umbrella, she marched and yelled in the street, 'I'm not a member of the Third World. What the hell is the Third World? God only made one world. I'm a member of that world!'

Typically divided in politics as in everything else my father who supported Manley said, 'See if you can get your mother off the street. Tell her to go into the Sheraton and have a cup of coffee or something.'

Untroubled by the communist threat he put a large picture of his advertising agency in the local newspaper with the headline, 'We're Staying.'

The following week, when something even more horrific than usual had taken place in a time of unprecedented alarm, he called a columnist, 'Maurice, last week I put an ad in saying, "We're Staying", Manley called to thank me. Well this week I'm running another "We're Stuck!".

Dawg nyam yu supper

Gossip was completely foreign to Mummy's nature. She

wouldn't indulge in it nor would she listen to it. Many times she would warn someone who had started to 'sus' in her car that they should stop. Of course, they wouldn't believe that there was anyone in the world who didn't like to hear 'how that one go' so they would speed up to get to the part that would tempt her to listen. She would stop the car and say, 'Now I've asked you to stop. I do not care about these people's business. If you persist I have to ask you to get out of my car.'

This revulsion was unique in a tiny place where everyone is constantly watching everyone else to the point that the desperation for an impossible privacy has become part of the language.

Suh, yu get through with that thing?

When I became an adult, we would have many discussions sitting in her kitchen in our nighties. She deplored my tendency towards guile.

'I spit on guile, I say what I think and damn the consequences!'

'But don't you see that, that way, you always win the battle but lose the war?'

'If I lose, I lose but I fight to the death.'

'Oh that's very fine, very noble, but some of us have to live out here in the real world, we can't afford your medieval code. Very often you are right but your behavior when you are right makes you wrong.'

'Right is right. Going along with what is wrong is collaboration.'

'Well look, you insult the policeman, let's leave out who was right and who was wrong. You give him your driver's license and drive off leaving him holding it. You sail away across your moat to your castle and you pull up the drawbridge and you spit away at the consequences from your tower. But your existence depends on some schmuck getting in a rowboat, soothing down the policeman and getting your license back. That schmuck was my father and now it's me. I resent it.'

Deep down though I wasn't so sure. There was something in that lack of compromise, the 'damn-the-consequences-attitude,' that people thrilled to in her.

It was tragic and unforgettable because it was rare. Maybe it was a zany Don Quixote type of courage but it was courage. I miss that complete lack of hypocrisy that disdain for popularity.

'I'm not trying to be a sweetheart of the whole damn world. You know exactly where you stand with me!'

Now she lives, inconveniently sometimes, in my bloodstream and surprises me by jumping out without warning when I need to defend myself. More and more as I get older and grapple with expediency, I appreciate in retrospect that fierce loyalty, that full one hundred percent. If she was on your side she was on your side, whether you were right or wrong.

4

Scotland

Learn fi dance a yaad before yu dance abraad

Scotland was to be a recurring theme in my life. It started with the new art teacher at school, Val Bloomfield, who in her short skirts and just out of the Glasgow School of Art, brought with her all the exciting, contemporary ideas of the outside world.

It must have been Val's idea to send a small group of precocious students, wearing our school uniforms, to draw from the model at the Art School on North Street in downtown Kingston. Life drawing is a thousand times more exciting than plant studies and I was lucky to have started it so early as it sparked an interest that was to be indelible.

The Art School was in a wooden colonial building, with polished floors, high ceilings and huge sash windows. It had a wonderful smell of paper and paint but had never had a graduate. Some of the students had been taking classes there for twelve years.

There was an amazing teacher, who had just arrived on the island, called Bill Broome, also trained in Scotland, whose brogue was almost unintelligible. Like a character out of D. H. Lawrence, who I was avidly reading at the time, he was a sculptor and a magnetic teacher mainly of woodcarving. He soon had all the young male students carving huge pubis shaped statues in wood with hollowed out sections, sprayed with bright colours rather like pregnant spoons. I thought they were marvelous – real modern art – and I bought one. Mine was an elongated pubis including stylised labia, topped with a couple of breasts going in different directions.

I later took my four-foot high carving with me to Scotland and, at my first digs, I always knew when the cleaning lady had been to tidy my room because she covered the outlandish object with a pillowslip every single time.

Bill Broome also taught life drawing and would stride up to the nude model, point at her hair, and announce, 'Blue black.'

He would point at her eyes, 'Black.'

He would point at her skin, 'Sombre burr-own.'

Then, seemingly overcome with emotion at her loveliness, he would stride out of the room shaking his huge head slowly from side to side in disbelief.

He recommended The Duncan of Jordanstone College of Art in Dundee to my parents. There was a teacher there, Hugh Adam Crawford, who he thought of highly. Unfortunately when I got to Dundee, Mr Crawford had been kicked upstairs into administration and was now the Principal of the Art school.

At this time in Jamaica, I was also taking extra classes with Barrington Watson who was a Slade graduate and a dazzling painter. There, again working from the nude, I imitated his super-sophisticated line drawings, like the little fifteen-year-old parrot that I was. On the strength of a portfolio of these quick drawings on newsprint – slick superficial imitations of the fashionable art school style – I was accepted into the College.

My mother bought my college clothes: my first winter coat; button down shirts; woolen jumpers and knee-high socks in New York. My clothes marked me at college, as if it wasn't exotic enough coming from Jamaica.

On this first trip to Britain, I remember sitting with my parents in a restaurant in London where we had stopped *en route* to Dundee. The waitress said 'Kew' under her breath every time she placed something on the table and it interrupted the flow of my father's conversation.

'What is she saying?'

'She is saying, thank you.'

'But why, I haven't given her anything yet?'

One thing was immediately clear, from the very first day, we certainly were not English.

Dundee is a small Scottish mill town on the banks of the River Tay. I found the cobbled streets, the dark stone buildings, the gloomy maze of tiny streets, and the bent over people grimly smiling in spite of the cold, strange and enchanting. The town looked to me like one of those pen and ink illustrations from a Victorian children's book.

I couldn't understand a word that they were saying because apart from the brogue the terms were so different.

'Shall I knock you up in the morning?'

Or the way commands were put: 'Would you like to chop wood in the greenhouse?'

'Why doesn't Anne', who was the landlady, 'just tell me to do it?', I would silently whine to myself. She must have known, of course, I wouldn't like to.

The code of politeness was another puzzle. In Jamaica we are not polite with intimates. We give an order: 'Get me some water nuh?'

The word 'nuh' softens the command. If we said to a close friend, 'Please would you get me some water', they would wonder why we were cold because politeness is associated with a formality that is reserved for strangers. If you had said, 'get me some water, nuh?', to anyone in Scotland they would gaze at you like Jesus looking at Judas in *The Arrest of Christ* by Giotto.

There was another Jamaican girl at the college, Christine, who was in her second year and I went to live at a little rooming house that she had pioneered. It was called The Grail and was reserved for overseas girls. Our landlady, Anne, was a cheery spinster who went to church every day and lived there too.

Christine was a Chinese Jamaican. She had been to boarding school in Kingston and was consequently much more independent than me and impatient with any coddling. The first day at school we had to take two buses to get there. To Christine's scorn I had never been on a bus. We went together but she told me to find my way back. Heart beating wildly I did it only to find my parents, like two mother hens, watching for me anxiously on the little lawn of 'The Grail.' I could see that when they left me they were reassured that the combination of Christine, 'The Grail' and Dundee made a safe place to leave their big baby. It was far away from the dangerous cities where one usually studied art such as New York, London or Paris.

I'm sure that they quarreled all the way home. When all four of the bed rooms of the little house filled up, I noticed that, in the shared bathroom, my name had been placed on the inside of the cupboard door where we each had a shelf for toiletries. Beside my name were the words 'Wednesday and Saturday.'

'What is that with my name on it in the bathroom?' I asked my guide and interpreter Christine.

'It's the bath list.'

'What is a bath list?'

'Wednesday and Saturday are the days that you can have a bath.'

'What? I don't understand. What? Twice a week?! I'll die.

I'll die of germs. That's filthy. I can't. No. It's impossible; I've never heard anything like that!'

'Are you quite finished?'

'Errrrr, yes.'

'You can have extra baths but you must pay two shillings and sixpence and leave the money on top of the cupboard.'

As a child of the tropics, I had thought nothing of having three baths a day. My culture shock had begun in earnest.

If someone gave you a cigarette or paid three pence for your ride on the bus you were expected to repay it by the end of the day. I ran a test and gave back a Kleenex to replace one that I had borrowed from one of the other girls. It was accepted. In Jamaica we would be insulted if you even thought something so small was remembered.

I made a thousand mistakes. I would run into a bakery and point at the loaf of bread I wanted, out of turn. The first time I did it I thought they were going to lynch me. I never did it again. One had to ask for things by their correct names, 'a small pan', or a 'husky brown' with no waving or pointing. Also you asked for it, when it was your turn, and only after a remark or two about the weather.

'Lovely day.'

'Aye, bit nippy.'

I learned that it was the worst possible form to complain. If one had a splitting headache one grinned and one bore it. A complaint would cause exchanged glances and a series of complaints would result in an explosive, 'Och, stop yer greeten lass!'

At home complaining and conversation were one and the same.

The cold was exciting although for the entire first year I didn't really feel it. The sheer novelty of putting a hot water bottle in the freezing bed to warm it before getting in and sitting close to the stove in the little 'lounge' as they called it to watch black and white television or bending over that one bar of heat on a sort of toaster in my room to get dressed, was all fun.

The first time I saw snow filled me with utter delight. The dark branches of the trees outlined in white and even the slipping and sliding as I tried to walk in slush, was hysterically funny to me.

One could walk on those cobbled streets at any hour with complete safety except for dodging the careening, vomiting drunks on Friday nights at closing time. I was deeply shocked by the drinking laws that so obviously encouraged drunkenness. The bell ringing loudly in the pubs caused desperation as people, with pints and pints of ale lined up on the table, frenziedly downed them all at the last minute.

'Time gentlemen, please. Time!'

'How late do the pubs stay open in Jamaica?'

'As long as anyone is drinking.'

Having a drink was an activity that was so natural at home – the first thing offered on entering anyone's house.

'Have a drink, man!'

'Gimme a rum and ginger, nuh.'

My father did not trust a man who did not drink so I found the guilty Scottish mystique surrounding it odd. And their pubs bored me. I consequently missed out on a big area of the social life of the students as it was centered round the pubs with most of the national humour rooted in drinking stories in the way that it centered around wife stories in America.

The food was completely tasteless to me at first. It was innocent of spices and pepper and in such small helpings. You could count the green peas on the plate, the tiny scoop of mashed potatoes with a bland meat pie, followed by milky coffee that tasted like tea.

I was not used to walking and no matter how hard I tried I couldn't walk as fast as the locals. It was as if they were on skates. After a month or two the shinbones of both legs hurt so much that I wrote home.

'Don't be alarmed but I think I have polio in my legs.'

My father sent a huge bouquet of flowers, enough to give to all the girls in the boarding house for their rooms, with a note that said, 'Cheer up, Darling.'

'Judy Ann, your father is like a lover not a father!'

I felt proud of him and desperately, desperately, homesick.

Whenever I thought of home, I would think of the evening sky with the strongly silhouetted shape of the mountains against it and the little kerosene lamps and how the people looked lit up in that light. I tried to paint it from memory.

The first sight that inspired a painting in my new world was a tiny park shrouded in mist with some workmen raking leaves. I painted it in watercolour and took it to the college. I nearly screamed when the teacher put the sheet of paper in the sink and opened the tap and with his palm flat, he roughly washed the surface of the painting reducing it to a very vague atmospheric image.

That did make it misty all right. The demonstration loosened me up. There was a blacksmith's shop that I glimpsed passing on the street and the interior was beautiful to me. I did some watercolours from memory, sitting on the floor in my room and took them to the college.

I loved the lilac in bloom and would carry a sprig around with me. But most of all, I loved the work. I loved the work so much, that I would stay until the college closed.

The art students were critical of everything and they got

their education free. I was paying for mine and so grateful for it. Until then it was Impressionism and the painting that followed immediately after that interested me most but from my first art history lecture the work of the Old Masters was brought to life for me.

The teacher was a famous painter in Dundee, James McIntosh Patrick. Then in his sixties, he wore tweed suits and waistcoats and looked more like a professor than a painter. He was not taken seriously by the students who jeered at the meticulous realism of his landscape paintings and his lectures and slide shows on 'The History of Art'. They treated his class as an opportunity to have a party, howling with laughter as if he was a stand-up comedian. He would completely ignore them and fasten his eyes on me delivering his lecture to the one absolutely ravenous sponge in the room that wanted every drop he had to give. His passion for the paintings became mine. That was what I had come for. I read Ernst Gombrich, Sir Herbert Read, Sir Kenneth Clark as well Newton and Ruskin from the college library.

I loved McIntosh's own paintings too. There were two in the Dundee museum that were unforgettable in the same way as the *View of Delft* by Vermeer – intense and without gimmicks they distilled the essence of a much loved place. One of them, painted in 1940, was called *The City Garden*. It showed his wife hanging out washing, helped by their daughter in his own back garden. Over the wall the factory buildings of Dundee are painted in fine detail. While the intricate drawing of the apple trees in front of the white sheets and the long shadows on the grass are so lovingly rendered that it is easy to empathise with the artist. It was easy to imagine that in that year 'Macky P', as we called him, loved his life. His other masterpiece is of the Tay Bridge and is the view painted from the studio in the front of his big stone house. I was very honoured to visit him there once.

He occasionally taught a painting class and I was fascinated to learn how to chalk a string tied to a pin stuck into a gessoed wood panel. One would then twang the string to get the perspective lines. Or how to use the exact measurement straight on the painting, a technique called 'eye-size', which would result in tiny paintings that were as accurate as those of the Dutch masters.

The only other teacher at the college who went against the prevailing political correctness of the time and taught a definite technique was an Australian called, Ron Stenberg. He could show you how to make objects look round by making the 'turn from the light' the darkest tone and fading out to a reflected light as the object went round the corner. This was useful for drawing the plaster cast copies of ancient Greek and Roman statues that we studied in our first year. I found it all fascinating.

Mr Crawford, the great teacher who had taught Bill Broome, was the Principal of the College. Disappointed that he wasn't teaching, I had the audacity to knock on the door of his office, introduce myself and ask for his opinion on some drawings. He so loved teaching that he spoke to me for a long time and set exercises for me to bring back to show him. He even waved away the Head of the Painting Department who had knocked on the door during our conversation telling him to come back later.

One day in sculpture class, I noticed a little figure in plaster on a shelf near where I was working on my first head in clay. The figure had a hand up to its throat and was completely expressionist. It communicated pain and anguish and sent chills up my spine. I enquired who had done it.

'John Johnstone', came the reply.

Johnny was then in his fourth year. These aristocrats of the student body controlled the studios at the top of the building where they would drunkenly lurch through the corridors after the pubs closed and totally terrify timid little first year novices like me. Unnoticed by me, he was part of a particularly wild group one afternoon when I had the bad luck to be tripping along, like Little Red Riding Hood on her way to see Grandma, in the corridor on the top floor. My knee high socks and neat little mock kilt was enough to enrage the leader of the pack who gave me a violent kick from behind that sent me flying and sent all of them into howls of drunken laughter. But Johnny told me afterwards that he was ashamed of the attack by his big bear of a friend and moved by my distress.

He was brilliant and already legend in the college. The administration recognized his talent and he won everything they had to offer: a Post Diploma year with his own studio; and the following year a traveling scholarship to go wherever he wanted in Europe. He was skeletally thin and wore a rumpled black suit, the jacket of which he would turn around back to front, for the college dances that they called 'Hops'. I didn't find them fun because I've never been a drinker and the idea was to get drunk as possible and pass out. Johnny was drunk just about all the time and surpassed everyone in the school at passing out.

I was already in love with his work. I was sixteen and I thought he was a living genius. I stole the gold filter of his black Russian cigarette butt from the ashtray at the pub and he asked me to the pictures. I was in love for the very first time.

John was an ex-anorexic and as tortured a soul as anyone in a Herman Hesse novel. Yet when he invited me home to his family's house in Forfar, which was a short bus-ride from Dundee, I found to my great surprise that his family was completely conventional, golf-playing, dog walking people. His parents and one older and one younger brother lived in a lovely country house called Langlands, which became my archetype for houses in the country.

I adored the many weekends I spent there, sleeping in a huge pink guest room with windows looking out on the garden. The garden itself was full of brand new joys for me, among them, picking strawberries. Sent out with a basket by his mother, I would squat in the strawberry patch and find the huge, glowing fruit under the leaves and eat and eat and eat, coming in with an empty basket. I loved the homemade strawberry jam that Mrs Johnstone made. It was so much better than commercial jam and I can taste it now. At their house, I started to enjoy the food of Scotland: the thick lentil soups and the taste of plain boiled potatoes freshly dug up. Tomatoes and lettuce grew in the greenhouse and raspberries along the back wall. Years later, when I lived at my own country house, eating food straight from the earth would be one of my greatest pleasures.

After my first Sunday lunch there, Mrs Johnstone said the magic word 'walk' and the Labradors ran up with their leashes in their mouths. Walk? I was thinking of having a nap. 'My' Labrador hauled me along, as if on skis, at a furious clip all the way around his familiar route of the nearby loch. How strange I thought. In Jamaica dogs walked themselves. They also stayed outdoors. One of our dogs, having only ever heard the word 'outside' from my mother would come running because he thought it was his name.

In the attic were stacks and stacks of Johnny's drawings. He tried every style – one day Picasso, the next Kokoschka. He was an amazing draughtsman then and still is today. He drew the whole family watching television in the 'lounge' – the room, the dogs, everything. His paintings were thick outpourings of passion in wild brush strokes, the paint unmixed, straight from the tube. The subject matter was dire though: the destruction of the world; 'the bomb'; evil overcoming good; human suffering and all the concerns of the young in the sixties. I was very influenced by his expressionist style and in a way it slightly threw me for a while from the realism that was always my natural bent.

It was on my first summer holiday home from Scotland that I saw my country for the first time with eyes no longer innocent – critical eyes that were able to compare. I had accepted as completely natural the black woman sleeping on a cot in the bedroom that I shared with my brother as a child. When I opened my eyes in the world she was there. She told us *Anansi* stories and riddles:

'Jack Mandora, guess me dis riddle an praps not!

Jack Mandora! Jump on de wire! De wire ben!

An dat is how de story en!'

She told us about Brother Tookuma and filled me with terror of lizards that would fly into my hair and get so entangled there that all my hair would have to be cut off to get them out. In one year away from the only reality I had ever known new attitudes, new judgments, imprinted on my young mind indelibly. I was changed by those years in Scotland, they made me slightly odd at home, a little out of step and that was to be permanent.

On my first holiday back, when my parents picked me up at the airport, I was decked out in white lace stockings and very short skirt à la Mary Quant and their voices sounded slow and thick and sleepy.

'Did-you-have-enough-mun-ee, dar-ling?'

To my horror I heard a never before used word come out of my mouth.

'Oh scads!'

My brother gave me a murderous look in the back of the car

and I didn't blame him. My parents were pleased.

'What-a-way-she is speaking nicely. Lovely, man.'

It was ecstasy to be home: the caress of the air in the morning; the loud noise of the insects at night; the sound of water dripping on leaves; the shifting light; the searing heat; the street life and the street calls.

'Pean-ert! bubble-gum, mint-stick, guava- cheese, chack-lit?'

'Chack-lit far de lady?'

I painted all summer and when, thirty years later, I saw again a still life from that summer of tropical fruits, the image was so happy that it catapulted me back like a time machine to my youth and my utter joy to be back home.

In my second year Christine and I were joined by a third Jamaican and we all rented a flat together. Angela was one of the most beautiful people I ever saw in my life. She was Lebanese, tall, with jet-black hair and eyes and a preference for wearing bright colours. She looked like a tropical flamingo in grey Dundee. She cooked the most incredible meals that tasted of home and reduced the Scottish boys to whimpering masses. Our flat was big and shabby. There were huge over stuffed armchairs with clouds of dust that would arise from the arms when we slapped them sometimes in laughter. The sitting room had a bay window view of the River Tay. And across the water there were the rolling hills of that most romantic sounding of places, The Kingdom of Fife.

We three West Indians were downstairs and four English girls were up the stair. The bathroom was on their floor and we were shocked that they shared bathwater among other strange habits. We all used the kitchen which had a couple of gas stoves called 'cookers' and a pulley hoisted a clothesline above our heads with washing that dripped for a week before it dried because it was so cold. In the morning the water from the tap crippled my hands and leaving the heated living room to sit on an ice-cold toilet seat had to be put off until the bladder was bursting. We each got a pound of shillings a week for the various metered electric fires. The rent was four pounds a week, which left six pounds from my budget of ten for everything else. Entertainment was having coffee, with exotic additions of marshmallows and dancing to gramophone records especially to Trini Lopez, 'Unchain my HEART, Baby set me FREE!' Then as the night wore on came jazz: Thelonius Monk; Miles Davis; Dave Brubeck; Bessie Smith and Lester Young. Often we stayed up all night talking and listening to that new prophet of our generation, Bob Dylan, before going off to College in the morning without sleep.

In my fourth year at art school I took an evening class in printmaking and fell under the spell of a new process that distracted me from painting. Etching fascinated me because no matter how long you worked on a plate you won't see what you are producing until the print is pulled. Getting the surprise is like an addiction. You want it again. One by one the other students in the class drifted away and then finally the teacher himself. He said he was only one page ahead of me in Stanley William Hayter's book about printmaking anyway and so he simply gave me the book. The college offered me a Post Diploma year to do etching but I declined.

My relationship with Johnny had no future partially because he had fallen under the influence of that somewhat depressing faction of religious life, The Jehovah's Witnesses. I believed in God but that seemed far away from the bizarre beliefs of this group and although I didn't have the strength to fight them, I certainly couldn't join them. I was twenty and life beckoned. I tore myself away from Scotland and Johnny and went home to Jamaica. I was still a virgin.

5

Back Home

Tidey fi me tomorrow fi yu

Going home for good was different from going home on holiday. I didn't have any idea what to do next. I wanted to be an artist but felt that my parents had already done a lot for me and I didn't want to ask them for more support, so I got a job teaching art at The Queen's High School for Girls.

I could walk to work as it was just up the road from our family house. Like Val Bloomfield before me, I was just a little older than my students. Full of enthusiasm I threw myself into teaching but as anyone who has done it knows, teaching is a selfless task requiring a great deal of dedication.

Everything that I wanted to paint myself I assigned to the students. Although I enjoyed teaching and got satisfaction in getting most of the students through their exams, I had no energy left over for my own work. Also, if I had not still been living at home – roofed, fed and clothed by my parents – I couldn't have done it because I was getting four pounds and ten shillings a week, which was exactly the same pay as our poor illiterate old gardener, Roy.

Suh, who is your Daddy?

My father suggested that I come to work for him at MacMillan Advertising Ltd.

When I first arrived the staff there were glad, imagining that with all that art school training I would be a big help.

'We have boys here who haven't even finished high school!'

I was completely and utterly useless.

I had spent four years perfecting an expressive line, a thick and thin line that was full of life. I tried to improve the layout they gave me, which is a big no-no. They want it just the way it is. I got on better by just tracing it. The boys who hadn't finished high school could do the job. I couldn't. The head of the art department was a man from New York called Jimmy Forbes. He stood at my drawing board all day cracking jokes with that famous New York humour.

'Jimmy, Help me, I'm hopeless at this.'

'I don't wanna help ya Judy, I want ya to get ouda here and paint!'

Finally I met my Waterloo in the form of a shoe-bag, which had to be designed by that afternoon as the client was coming to see it at four o'clock. The design was simply brown and white stripes with a black and white logo, which one of the boys were going to do. I only had to do the stripes.

With a setsquare, a T-square and a drawing board all my stripes converged towards the ends of the paper.

'Jimmy, for God's sake, tell me how to do it!'

'Hey Judy just stick a piece of brown paper over the white paper with cow gum and cut the stripes out with a Stanley knife and peel them off. It's easy!'

All my stripes frayed along the edges when I tried to peel them off. There was no possibility of meeting the deadline.

I went into my father's office.

'I'm quitting before you fire me. I wasn't trained for this. I'm very conscious that I've lasted five weeks in here only because I'm the boss's daughter.'

'Meet me on top of the State this evening at six o'clock.'

His habit was to drink a bottle of whisky every evening on

the roof of his cinema with a court of cronies. I was certainly a blank canvas when I arrived for that summit meeting but it is one of the moments that changed the course of my life. I've always been grateful to him because he made a deal with me and it was an honourable deal.

'Look, what can you do? You can't do shorthand and typing even though you had a secretarial course.'

That was after high school and before college with the result that I could write 'Dear Sir' in Pitman's Shorthand, nothing more.

'You can't teach because you would starve to death. You can't do advertising. It seems to me that the only thing you've ever been good at is painting. So, why don't you paint?

I said nothing and he went on.

'I'll make a deal with you. I'll give you ten pounds a week for a year. You have had office experience now, so do it like an office job. You go into your studio (this was the garage at home) at nine, you work until five. You don't work on weekends. Your end of the deal is, you must produce a one-man show.'

Oh the sweet relief of that moment. A clear and shining path opened up in front of me. I could definitely do that.

Better than that, I did it in six months!

My first show in Kingston was in the bar of The Colony Club now reincarnated as a gallery. The frieze by Alvin Marriott was painted white and it made the room distinctive. Mr Carter, the best lighting man in Kingston, who had lit parties and many concerts for my father installed spot lights that did not bleed colour. The invitations were done at MacMillan Advertising in black and white. On the cover was a self-portrait of a serious young woman who is declaring herself an artist. Mrs Edna Manley, herself an artist and the wife of the Premier Minister, opened the show. It differed dramatically in style from most exhibitions in Kingston up till then. Totally unlike one of those dreary little morning gatherings downtown at the Institute of Jamaica with everyone clutching a hot rum punch in a paper cup. This was like a cocktail party when my father, 'Mr Show Business', decided to launch his daughter. He did everything he could for me except paint the pictures.

Parson christen him pickney fus

There were thirty paintings – mainly portraits and nudes and street scenes from my imagination of higglers sleeping on the street. These higglers fed Jamaica. They would carry the huge flat baskets of yams and vegetables that they had grown on their heads over the Blue Mountains, all the way from the North Coast or the rugged interior of the island, singing as they walked. They would sleep on the sidewalks for the weekend going back over the mountains on Sunday with light baskets.

While working for that first show, I had seen a most imposing older Rasta man who I wanted very much to paint. I also wanted to talk to him, as I had never had a chance to speak to a Rasta. There were melodramatic speculations in the 1950s about how they would become 'inflamed' on ganja and, with eyes as red as dragons, chop off one's head with a machete. But this man looked as calm and dignified as a king.

I sneaked him into my garage studio under the radar of my mother's eyes.

His name was Daniel Emmanuel Malcolm McEwan and he wore a diadem on his head and many paintable emblems that enhanced his wonderful graying locks. Anticipation high, I began a portrait and as always when I am very excited by a subject, it started well.

I cringe to remember but I opened conversation with, 'So … what do 'You People' believe in anyway?'

'We believe in racial equality and black supremacy.'

Unable to see any clear path through these entirely conflicting concepts I said, 'I don't believe that revolutions solve anything, because usually the oppressed become the oppressors'.

Looking towards Beverly Hills, a screaming new residential area above Kingston he said, with a little back and forth inverting gesture of one hand, 'That may be but it's time for a likkle change-up now.'

When the paintings were framed and hung my father priced them to fly off the walls and they did. It was a sellout show except for one that was given to Mrs Manley to thank her and one other, of a man standing on the back of a truck, that did not sell.

I took all of the money and went to New York with my mother spending every cent of it.

When I came home my father said, 'What are you going to do now?'

'I'm going to do it again.'

I never spent all the money again though.

I always tell young painters that you have two arts to master. One is your painting and that is difficult enough. But selling your paintings is another and if you are to stay the course it is equally as important. At this time I also got my first government commission. The government commission, as many artists will tell you is a minefield so dangerous that it can ruin a career before it begins and that nearly happened with mine. Mr Edward Seaga was the Minister of Finance and I was asked to meet him at the Ministry office to discuss a commission.

Scared to death, I listened politely as he told me that he wanted a portrait of Sir Donald Sangster who had been Prime

Minister of Jamaica. As the gentleman was dead I was just opening my mouth to say that, 'No, regrettably I only painted from life' when he mentioned that the fee was three hundred pounds. Three hundred pounds! My God, I thought, for that I would paint Attilla the Hun and he had been dead for centuries. There is a price that drives all anxiety about prostitution out of mind, so I said yes and the rest of our discussion centered around the size. I said, 'Head and hands?'

This is a portrait term for the standard size, which is just below life-size to avoid that gross heroic scale associated with propaganda. I thought we were on the same page, as the Americans say and off I went.

As I had been in Scotland the whole time that Sir Donald Sangster was Prime Minister I had never actually seen the man. I watched film footage. I studied the colouring of members of his family. I got the official photograph that showed him seated at his desk and I painted my twenty-year old heart out for one month. Before delivering it, I showed it to members of his family and they declared with eyes wet that it was, 'Him to the life!'.

Satisfied, I left the portrait at the office of the Minister of Finance and nothing happened for a very long time. No response. Finally I called, to be told that a 'mistake' had been made. It turned out that they wanted a full length standing portrait. What about payment though for the one I had done? No response.

Broken with disappointment, I took to my bed. After I had cried for a few days my mother got into her car and drove down to the Ministry of Finance. Without an appointment she walked into the office in full Catherine of Russia style.

'Tell Mr Seaga that I have come for my daughter's money.'

'You can't come in here without an appointment.'

'Oh you think so? Listen, I'll come in here anytime I damn well choose. Mr Seaga fooled up some poor illiterates and got himself put in here, well tell him VIDA MACMILLAN IS HERE TO PUT HIM OUT AND YOU BETTER BRING MY DAUGHTER'S MONEY RIGHT NOW IF YOU DON'T WANT A SERIOUS SCENE IN HERE TODAY.'

She returned home with the money.

'She a viraga!'

I decided that it took two to make a mistake and offered to paint the portrait again for no additional money, if they would specify the dimensions. A series of letters passed between Mr Seaga and my mother but she, as you may guess got the last word because when she wrote, 'Dear Mr Seaga please don't communicate with me anymore because you bore me utterly'. She received no more letters from him.

I never saw my second standing portrait of Sir Donald Sangster again. I expect it is rolled up in some dusty place where all those 'studies' by foreign experts are. Commissioned portraits are usually the worse paintings that you will see by Jamaican artists. They are only commissioned after death, as if the subjects are far too busy or too important to be bothered with time-wasting foolishness. Never mind the portraits of Kings, Emperors and Popes in the museums of the world in the days before cameras. These men were not as important as Jamaican politicians and insurance salesmen.

It was just around that time that something much more important happened. I met Dave.

Uh huh now. Story come to bump

I was as sick of being a virgin as it was possible to be and sick of the '50s doctrine and my mother's mantra, 'My dear, no decent man will marry a girl who has been used.'

'I don't want to get married.'

'What?'

'I don't think I want to get married.'

'What nonsense! No woman can be happy without a home, a husband and a family of her own. I may not have been happy but your father took one look at me and I was Mrs Dudley G. MacMillan three months later, and one thing I will always give him credit for he has been a damn good provider.'

Dave was an American engineer from Ohio. He had never left the United States before he came down with the original team to build the Goodyear Tire plant in Morant Bay. He had a little Volkswagen car, an apartment in Norbrook, a Zippo lighter that never failed, in fact everything he had worked and he was fond of saying, 'I don't hurt for anything.'

I met him through mutual friends who recommended me when he expressed the wish for a Jamaican painting for his apartment. Several instructions came via the grape vine until, finally, when I heard that he wanted a girl on a donkey it was on the tip of my tongue to fire off, 'Tell him to paint it himself!'

Luckily I didn't say that though, because just then, a beach party was arranged and I met him. He was tall, dark and 'movie-star' handsome with a devastating smile. He was wearing Bermuda shorts though and looked very American which after Scotland I was a little armed against, so I decided that he was just full of himself and I didn't like him. You will recognise the precaution here, it was just in case he didn't like me. After the beach party he drove me home and we stopped at his apartment where he cooked spaghetti and meat sauce. It was delicious and he didn't seem so full of himself after all.

We started 'dating'. Well, I had never been on dates before. In Scotland we went out in groups, paying for ourselves; there was no dating.

Dating was dressing up in an evening dress and a real man who had his own independent life coming to pick you up and taking you to dinner or a nightclub. This was grown up stuff. I loved it and my mother was over the moon.

He was exactly what she had in mind for me.

Dave liked to dine at Blue Mountain Inn and always ordered the Chateaubriand. One evening I had gone to a cocktail party before our dinner date and heard this English Brigadier, big moustache, you know the type; speaking very knowledgeably it seemed to me about wine. I asked him to advise which wine to go with our dinner later and he said, 'Chateau Lafitte'.

How will I ever remember that I wondered?

'Oh just think of feet,' he said, looking at mine.

Later when the wine waiter came I looked down and said, 'Chateau la Feet.'

I should have suspected something when the waiter murmured as he slipped away, 'She has good taste.'

It might as well have been a flat Coke to us.

When we were driving down the hill though, Dave was even more quiet than usual.

'What's wrong?'

'Nothing.'

He looked a bit green around the gills.

'No, something's wrong, please tell me.'

'I couldn't believe the bill that's all.'

'You must query it. Maybe there's been a mistake!'

I waited in the car and he went in. When he came out and drove down the hill he said, 'It was the wine.'

At least we had closure but after that we waved wine waiters away decisively!

Dave really enjoyed his adventure in Jamaica, despite the fact that everyone he met, hearing that he was from Goodyear immediately said that the tires were no good and that they exploded on the road. It was classic Jamaican style to denigrate passionately anything made on the island. He thought nothing of driving even as far as Negril for the day and we explored the whole island in his little Volkswagen.

He was nine years older than me and had not met a virgin in years. I decided that he definitely was the one to rid me of my burden. After all, he looked like a romantic hero in the movies and he was an experienced man who wouldn't botch it. Tired of saying 'no', I wanted to say, 'come on let's go.' Well, Dave was happy to oblige but I don't think he expected to fall in love with me.

When my grandfather died some time later and I was standing with my family in the church at his funereal. I heard the distinctive engine of his little car arrive all the way from work in Morant Bay. To an audible gasp from my family he entered the church, strode over to me in the pew and took my hand. I knew in that moment that he loved me.

'Oh my, nice eh? What a lovely man, an they look lovely togedder.'

We had been 'dating' for about two years when my mother asked him on the verandah one evening what exactly were his intentions towards me. He said an unfortunate thing.

'Judy Ann and I enjoy each other.'

She got up and walked inside and when he left she went off like the atom bomb.

'ENJOY? This di-yam American has the nerve to tell me he is ENJOYING my daughter????? EH???? He is COMPLETELY out-of-order. A piece of di-yam impertinence.'

He was a dead duck in the water to her after that. Shortly after, his time in Jamaica was up and he left to go back to Ohio. He missed me, called and said on the phone, 'Let's get married.'

I wanted to continue the relationship and to get married was the only way. 'Living in sin' as they called it then was out of the question, so I said yes.

My father took me to Miami to shop for my trousseau because they were quarrelling again. I bought my wedding dress at Jordan Marsh which was a nice department store and also some of those Lacoste knit dresses and a blue blazer for my honeymoon and to start life in Ohio.

My mother now approved of Dave again and planned the wedding with joy. His family, father, mother and twin brother came down and it was the last event that took place in that Deco house at West Avenue where I had grown up.

I spent the day itself with my hair in curlers rolling little cotton wicks for the tiny clay dishes that my mother had bought and which were placed all over the garden and in the hedges all the way up the long driveway.

'Just like the festival of lights!'

Sporadically I used to go out with a Norwegian who called me that week.

'Are you busy on Saturday night?'

'Yes. I'm getting married.'

When I walked down the aisle on my father's arm he was speechless with shock to hear me muttering as if in a trance, 'What am I doing here? What am I doing here?'

Abe Issa and Norman Manley, the Prime Minister at the time, made speeches at the reception. The wedding party wore white and my little sister and her best friend were bridesmaids.

We had a short honeymoon in Jamaica in a hotel on the North Coast and then flew off to the United States – first to Miami where he collected his car and on to Williamsburg and Washington.

'I want to show you where this country began.'

We drove up to Ohio in Dave's brand new red Sting Ray Corvette on expressways.

'GAS FOOD LODGING PHONE AHEAD GAS FOOD LODGING PHONE AHEAD. GAS FOOD LODGING.'

'I'd love to see some of the country.'

'Well this is West Virginia. We wanna get through here as quickly as possible.'

'Why?'

'Dry State.'

I saw no discernible change in the terrain when he suddenly said, 'Look at those trees … Ohio.'

'Darling don't you think you should go and look at the place before you decide to live there?'

'Oh no Daddy, we love each other.'

My first sight of Akron from the expressway was an unforgettable shock. The Goodyear factory looked like those dark satanic mills, red brick with green glass windows and black smoke belching from tall chimneys. He said, 'There's where I work.'

It looked like hell on earth to me. From the heart I said, 'Oh, you poor darling,' and too late realised that he was showing the Goodyear factory to me with pride.

I glanced behind and saw a big truck coming up fast on the expressway. I thought if I open this door and jump out it will be all over really quick. I would be squashed flat like Olive Oyle in the comics and not have to live here.

We arrived at his mother's house and entered, American- style, through the back. Esther, his mother, and Will, his father, had been in Jamaica for the wedding and she had needed tranquillisers to drive up a hill that wasn't very steep by Jamaican standards, to the hotel where they stayed. Here she was at the sink making a salad to go with dinner and I stood in the kitchen watching as she shoved all the cuttings down, what looked to me, like the drain. I had never seen a garbage disposal unit and although I had heard of them, somehow imagined that they were outside in the garbage can.

I was thinking: Well, I'm too polite to mention it but *boy* is she going to have a clogged drain when suddenly she flipped a switch and the thing loudly gobbled up the cuttings. I screamed and leaped back across the room.

After dinner we went to our house. It was a modern apartment with wall-to-wall carpeting and sliding glass windows that looked at each other across a small courtyard. I often wished, while living there, that I could have blown a hole through that courtyard wall so that I would be able see out and feel that life had prospects. I was delighted to have a garbage disposal of my own and fed mine eggshells and by mistake several of the silver wedding spoons, which were mangled. The only furniture was a bed. He had waited for me to shop for our furniture and soon we had a huge soft sofa as well but not much else. When my mother visited she said, 'Wonderful! You live such uncluttered lives!'

No one ever came to see us and we went to see no one. After several weeks I asked, 'Don't you have any friends?'

An evening was arranged to meet his friends and I mean arranged: cross country journeys; sitters; time schedules; venues. I dressed as I would have to go to a hotel or restaurant in Kingston – black satin mini-skirt, white evening blouse, teased hair, make-up including false eye-lashes and a cigarette holder. When we entered the restaurant a group of people were in the way and I was looking beyond them when it turned out that these were them, his friends. Scrubbed faces, linen dresses mid-calf, I immediately felt like the Whore of Babylon.

The men on arrival disappeared to the furthest spot they could reach at the bar leaving us women in a cluster. Conversation began with a shriek from one of the women loud, and I mean loud.

'Guess what I did today!'

I leaned forward.

'I bought a pair of bell bottoms!'

Shock registered on my face and she continued, 'Well I guess that isn't anything to you Judy but it's very exciting to me.'

Conversation focused mainly around techniques for cleaning things.

'I get down there and I scrub that floor good before waxing it.'

Or cooking things like casseroles, chicken divan and baked beans.

'Judy Ann, when are you going to become an American citizen?'

'Errr, well, I'm not a refugee.'

Little did I know then, that I was soon to be one because the Michael Manley years were coming up.

My first party in Akron was an odd experience. There was no sound of music when we approached but at the back the party was in full swing. Everyone was wearing nametags and before we were even offered a drink we were urged to join one of two teams that were playing games. The games involved a blindfolded man feeling the knees of all the women who were seated in a row to facilitate this. He had to select his wife's knees from the knees of the other women in the row.

Another game was to burst a balloon by crushing it against one's opponent on the other team. They were all touchy-feely games and the winning team got candy.

At the end of a month I am ashamed to say I headed home. There was total disapproval at home for this cowardly move.

'Darling, marriage is trying and you have not even begun to try.'

Mea culpa. I went back determined to try.

To avoid being a social outcast you had to play golf, bowling and bridge.

I decided to try the bridge. I was hopeless at bridge but l enjoyed being 'dummy' so that I could get away from the table and serve the coffee on our exquisite Wedgwood china from our brand new wedding booty on top of all the Jamaican embroidered linen. One woman who was fashionably dressed but had a voice like a buzz saw screeched, 'Judy, do you have natives in Jamaica?'

While I gathered my thoughts on this one and before I could come up with an answer, another squawked, 'I wanna see you get yourself out of this one Madge.'

'Well, I am a native of Jamaica, but if you mean do we have black people in Jamaica yes, but if you mean do we have savages in Jamaica, no.'

My panic about Akron was compounded by the discovery from the very first month that I was pregnant. How many times have I thanked God that it happened so quickly because had it not, I would never have had Alexei.

6

Alexei

Still wata run deep

It felt like a fish, the subtle movement inside me that whispered the reality of a child in my body. Towards the end of the waiting and growing I became suddenly filled with urgency to create a nest for the baby and threw myself into the selection of baby furniture and the perfect mobile for over the crib. The guest bedroom which, had never had a guest, became a nursery and I would glance into it as I passed in the passage way satisfied with the light and colours in the room. I painted one still life of pink and white dogwood for it – the only painting that I did in Ohio. Underneath these preparations though I was caught up in my panic to find myself unhappy and worse than that, I was ashamed of it.

I was expected to be really happy having achieved what all sensible Jamaican girls presumably would consider success: a nice American man who takes you to the mainland and who was, in my mother's words, 'Good husband material and a di-yam good provider.'

Dave, of course, knew better because I cried a lot. I was grieving for my life which I saw as disappearing down, down, down into an unending repetition of matching socks – the blue one with the blue one and, oh yes, that striped one with the other striped one. Life in America, notwithstanding the crispy lettuce, the family packs of chops in the supermarket, the shiny appliances and looking forward to a nice television set, could not make up for the loss of seeing a thousand things to paint with one roll of my eyeballs. The continuous visual stimulation that was such a huge part of my inner life had gone.

It was beyond homesickness. It was bereavement. How could my well-intentioned mother-in-law who loved her home as much as I did mine, know that her pleasant remark as we watched the Fourth of July Parade, 'Soon the baby will be marching in the parade,' would trigger in me the pure panic of a life sentence. Or that every time we passed a cemetery I imagined my tomb, having died a hundred years later with matching socks and casseroles my only creations.

The traumatic arrival of Alexei blasted out of existence all these concerns with the self.

When the bull enters the arena in Spain bursting with life and fiercely beautiful (which I had seen on holiday while at college) was how he looked to me. I completely forgot myself in the astounding reality of his actual presence and his vocal rage at being disturbed. He was a big baby, with huge shoulders the nurses said and the birth had been extremely difficult due to the simple fact that I was paralysed with fear.

It took thirty-six hours and when it was over my hair had 'locksed' into a matted clump far in advance of the fashion for dreadlocks. My teeth chattered uncontrollably in my head. There was truly no possibility of ever doing it again. Yet when they put him in my arms I wept with real joy and felt as if my heart would burst with love.

My mother was in Akron for the birth and I heard her little crocodile skin pumps coming up the corridor before she swept into the room, looking exactly like a Latin American Eva Gabor, wearing a black mink pillbox hat.

'Darling, darling, darling what a beautiful baby boy. Oh

Thank God, Thank God, Thank God, Thank God.'

When Alexei was ten months old I fled from Ohio with him. My American friends always say that my entire subsequent life was a reaction to that experience of culture shock in America's heartland. The example of a bad marriage that I had seen growing up had ended in divorce at home. I could not imagine succeeding where they had failed. All I could think of was to run and keep running so that the unhappiness I associated with marriage would never happen to me.

At the divorce I wore a red felt cowboy hat that had to be removed. You cover your head in an English court but uncover it in America.

The judge reminisced, 'Jamaica? Hey, my wife and I had our honeymoon "down there" and we had ourselves one hell-uva time out there in that wadder.'

It was all amicable because, you won't believe this, but I loved Dave very much and it felt terrible to hurt him. I took all the blame for the failure and felt enormous guilt and still do that I wasn't able to be his wife. We remained friends and as time went on I appreciated him more and more. Also I felt grateful to him for loving me enough to marry me and we had a bond for life in Alexei.

If I had been afraid of marriage before I was now in full flight. Also I had evidence. I had tried it my mother's way and it didn't make me happy. I now made an informed choice.

I was going to be a painter. I would give my child a happy mother. Work for my second exhibition started immediately.

One brief attempt to live under my mother's roof though proved that that you can never go home again. My mother often went to one of the hotels in New Kingston where Dave and I used to dance on Friday evenings to 'Strangers in the Night' or 'The Green, Green Grass of Home'. Between sets there was a floorshow and the dancers used the public Ladies room to get ready for the show. One night their manager, whom I knew said, 'Judy why don't you paint my girls?'

I couldn't believe my luck and these girls became my models. Madame Sugar Hips was a favourite with her pale brown skin. For painting from life really anyone will do and I find everyone interesting but it's a nice bonus if the models are as beautiful as these were.

'You did that?'

'What?'

'You look at a naked woman and paint 'ar?'

'Yes.'

'I coulda nevah do dat.'

'Why?'

'I couldn't look at a naked woman suh long.'

'Well, I'm afraid you couldn't paint her then, because it's the only way to do it.'

The West Avenue house had been demolished and a development with lots of small houses replaced it. My parents lived apart. My mother's house was now a large new residence in the hills above Kingston and there was a big room under the kitchen, which became a studio for me.

The studio had no bathroom attached and inevitably one or other of the dancers would have to pad through the house to my bedroom which was first door on the right after the obligatory wrought iron gate that locked off the bedroom section – as is usual in most Jamaican houses.

My routine was hectic because my mother refused to allow me a maid. So I had to wash all the baby's diapers and hang them out to dry. There were no paper diapers in those days and no diaper service either. Then I would put Alexei in his crib in my room to have his morning nap and jump into the car and hurl down to Trench Town in the depths of Kingston or some such locale, collect my model, race home and get an hour or so done before the baby's first cry. This usually signaled the end of painting for the day. I learned to paint with lightning speed.

One day my mother came in and met one of my models in the living room coming back from my bathroom in her dressing gown. I heard a shriek of outrage from upstairs.

'This is INTOLERABLE. I will NOT have these women with syphilis and gonorrhea using the toilets in this house!'

I nearly died of embarrassment. I wished the earth would divide in two and open up and swallow me. When I had taken the poor girl home, I tried to have it out with my mother.

'She was using my personal toilet which I clean.'

'This is my house and I will decide what goes on in here and I say NO.'

'But if I cannot ask a leper, or a beggar off the street or a prostitute or whoever I choose to use a toilet THAT I CLEAN, then I have no human rights.'

'HUMAN RIGHTS? HUMAN RIGHTS? You don't have any HUMAN RIGHTS. THIS IS MY HOUSE.'

'Well, I can't live without human rights.'

Sobbing I threw Alexei into the car and drove off down the hill.

I got a tiny one-bedroom flat, hired my very first helper and Alexei, Norma and I started life together. I truly felt that I had had my chance at happiness during my marriage and hadn't measured up. I would bring up my child, do my work and do my duty. Love and romance were over for me.

I threw myself into my career and motherhood. I was twenty-four.

Alexei and I were inseparable. We went most weekends to a cottage my family owned at Duncan's on the north coast.

Alexei and I would walk from one end of the beach to the other and play the same little games each time.

'Is this your house? Can I come in?'

After a year in the tiny flat we went to live at a wonderful old wooden house, which later became the Bob Marley museum on Hope Road. It had been split up into large flats and ours had louvre windows and high ceilings. It felt good on the skin and Alexei began to talk more there. Our neighbour was a rough diamond called Bap who lived in a flimsy shack on a piece of open land. He raised goats and Alexei would call over the fence to him and be lifted over into this interesting place with goats running everywhere and sometimes he would fall asleep over there in Bap's shack. One morning I went over.

'Hello. I'm the baby's mother. I see that he likes to come over here and I hope that he is not disturbing you?'

'I would never take revenge on an infant.'

Revenge? My hair literally stood on end.

'Ahhh, well revenge wasn't what I had in mind. I just wondered if he was bothering you?'

'No ah love de baby and what is more ah love de baby madder. I love yu becaw aldo you are tall, you seem to be quite fleshy.'

After that I didn't worry when he went to Bap's house.

At Alexei's first sports day he came dead last in the lime and spoon event. I mean he strolled in long after the race was finished with a completely indifferent look on his face. I thought that he hadn't noticed that he was in a race. My brother rolled his eyes and said, 'Well, your son has not exactly distinguished himself at sports today!'

Later when I tucked him in Alexei said, 'Mom, yu see how when I came last I didn't cry?'

I was astonished and moved that the little man had learned so early to cover his emotions.

He was not a talker and when he did speak it was in a downtown Kingston accent I never corrected in case it would inhibit him more. So, after visiting his American cousins in the summer he came back with, 'Dey say I talk funny.'

'What did you say?'

'I say dey talk funny too.'

'Good.'

When the children at school teased him.

'Dey call me "Sexy Alexei".'

'You won't believe this now but there will come a time when you won't mind that but tell me, what are their names?'

'One is Roger Mamoud.'

'Call him Roger Baboon.'

I would tell him often that I gave him the name Alexander because it means 'Leader of Men'. But he was never ever to care about popularity. He was never to follow, always to lead and never be afraid to stand alone. I taught him to have good manners.

'Alexei, if you ever see a woman carrying a metal chair across a church yard in high heels (as had just happened to me of course) and you don't find yourself on your feet instantly to help her you are not a gentleman. If you have to think about it, it is too late.'

When he was four he was already trying to help me carry groceries and when he was older the minute he heard the car switch off he would call from a window.

'Mom, do you need any help?'

All the nonsense that is spoken about loss of freedom, the awesome responsibility, and the sacrifice that it takes to bring up a child were never true of me. There was never any sacrifice that wasn't completely outweighed by his smile, his growing love for me and his solid little body beside me in the car. From the first look of recognition when he looked into my eyes and knew that I was his mother we were bonded. I knew that I was having the great experience of my life and the one that I was born for.

That said though, it was hardly smooth sailing. He nearly burnt the house down.

We were living in a small two-bedroom townhouse in New Kingston and Dave, who had left Ohio after we left and was now posted for Goodyear in South America, was visiting us from Peru.

My mother, Dave and I were having a drink in the living room when we all heard Alexei upstairs in my bedroom saying, 'What did I did? What did I did?'

'Excuse me a minute. I'm just going up to see what he has gotten himself into.'

I froze halfway up the stairs because that 'sheet of flame' you have heard about was in my bedroom and Alexei was spinning around in front of it gibbering. I grabbed him and screamed so loudly that I was hoarse for a week. My townhouse was in the middle of a row so if my roof burnt down so would the other houses. My neighbours sprang into action. Someone called the fire brigade. Another leapt into the room with a wet hankie tied over his face (obviously an ex-boy scout) shouting, 'Start a bucket brigade!'

All hell and pandemonium broke loose. When the fire brigade came and hooked up their hose it sprang water from a thousand leaks. I heard, to my rage, Alexei shouting excitedly to his buddies out there, 'Here comes annadda one!'

He was enjoying it. I could have spanked him senseless. All my neighbours in the adjoining houses gathered in the yard outside as water raged inside, ruining my house completely. One neighbour said to my mother in that accusing tone one has to get used to in Kingston, 'Where were *you* when the fire started?'

'We were having a drink, where were you?'

Alexei knowing that it was forbidden to play with matches had concealed himself inside my clothes closet to do so and the flame had ignited some of my clothes. In two seconds it spread upwards. When it was over I did not own a stitch of clothing other than what I was standing in.

My mother said, 'Come up to my house, borrow my clothes and you two go to dinner just as if nothing has happened.'

That seemed an excellent idea so we did. Later, when Dave and I sat at the Terra Nova Hotel, Dave said to the waiter, 'Bring me a double martini, no, make that a triple.'

It had been quite an afternoon.

It seemed to me that Alexei mellowed after that but continued to enjoy 'surprising' me.

We visited his father many times in Peru and Brazil where I loved being 'Senora Russ-ell' for a while and certainly had an easier life in that role.

Life in Jamaica settled into the routine that surrounds children: the school run in the morning; then dashing out to nearby spots to paint as I had started landscapes by then but only working where I could get back quickly to collect him after school. Sports days followed sports days, until the graduating year.

'Mrs. Russell what do you think of Alexei being captain of the football team?'

'What? I didn't know,' turning to see his delighted smile that he had done it again. There was another surprise at the school-leaving concert.

I had been told by my great friend, the talented music teacher Mary Johns, that Alexei 'was musical'. Now I heard that clear, pure voice and realised why he had cringed whenever I attempted to sing.

After graduation Dave arranged for Alexei to go to a school in Hudson, Ohio, called Western Reserve Academy where he had a grandmother near by. The school specialised in grooming students for American Universities.

He had a rough start at the school because his assigned roommate was cold to him and then refused to room with him because he was Jamaican.

Alexei explained on the telephone, 'You see Mom he comes from an area called Shaker Heights where they all wear designer clothes all the time.'

'So?'

'So they look down on other people.'

'Oh, please tell your roommate that your Mother says that a snob from Ohio, is a contradiction in terms.'

The first boys who were friendly were the black ones who by contrast claimed him for the exact same reason that the snob rejected him. He said he never knew before how good it was to come from Jamaica because it made him feel special. He became quite an athlete and when I went to visit the school many of the students told me that he had written an essay about me that had been put in the school magazine. Typically enough he had not mentioned it but I wrote to the school and requested a copy.

Reading it was a revelation, I knew for the first time, from his viewpoint, what growing up with me was like and what that silent little boy was thinking. Among the many aspects of our life together he said this about my work: 'One day she sets her easel up in front of a swamp with birds flying over it and the next, in front of a child with red ribbons in her hair. I have never known what motivates her but I know it cannot be prevented.'

When I read it I got on my own hotline to God, 'Thank you God, you can take me anytime you like now, this is more than enough.'

Whenever I got depressed after that my friends would say, 'Judy, read Alexei's essay again and cheer up.'

Alexei graduated from Boston University *cum laude*. Dave and I had tears in our eyes when at the end of the ceremony they announced to the graduating class, 'Now we want you to face your parents and thank them for the sacrifice that they have made.'

A roar went up and all those mortarboards flew into the air.

No longer a child, it was a man who drove us around Boston and took me to the Isabella Stewart Gardner Museum. It was a man, who pointed out the bronze statue of birds poised for flight in front of the school and commented, 'Mom, they say that when a virgin is discovered at Boston University, those birds will fly.'

He went to Florida with his Dad, who was at that time, retired from Goodyear and re-married to a Chilean woman. My mother's opinion after visiting them was, 'Judy I wish I could tell you there was something wrong with her but I loved her. She is just like you!'.

He started work in a shipping company owned by a Jamaican, the father of a good friend from High School, Charlie Johnson. The first day of his new job two ships that he was routing on computer nearly crashed because he was writing a song in his head. As time went on he became more and more unhappy in Florida and I began to worry about him for the first time.

Although he was doing as was expected of him: getting promotions; wearing designer clothes; making his car payments and certainly pleasing his father. He was having his first crisis. He felt trapped – moving forward on a road that did not satisfy his soul but he had not had the time to discover what would.

'What do you really want to do?'

'I want to go to Asia.'

He had already travelled a great deal from childhood, culminating in a long journey through Europe on his own some years before. He sold his car. I gave him the fare to London and my dear friend Christine, who had pioneered art school in Scotland, got him a job painting walls, which earned him the spending money. They sent a photo of him triumphantly holding a spread fan of paper bills and then, he disappeared for almost a year. There were a few postcards. The first one, from New Zealand said, 'I think this is where God takes his vacations.'

The odyssey ended in India where the postcards mentioned rail journeys in 100 degrees of heat. At long last we heard that he was coming back. I flew to Miami for the return of 'the Prodigal Son'. There was a knock on the door of his father's house and there he was standing on the doorstep with long tangled hair and a skimpy Fu Manchu moustache, which, it took a lot of restraint not to comment on – a restraint helped by the sure knowledge that one comment and we would be stuck with it for years.

I felt shy of him and sat gingerly on the sofa beside him because he was so strange. Now completely vegetarian, to his steak loving Dad's dismay, he drifted beside me in Dadeland Mall palpably emanating the world that he had just left and looking completely cut off from the one that we were in.

'Wait, suh what happen … him gawn off?'

My young guru came back to Jamaica with me. He was as calm and aloof as a Buddha but I won't lie to you, I was worried. However, faith is my strong point. I know how to wait in hope like Mr Micawber. That eternal optimist from *David*

Copperfield is not one of my heroes for nothing: 'I am absolutely certain that something of an agreeable nature will come up.'

One day not long after, he announced that he did not want vegetables that day and devoured two boxes of Kentucky Fried Chicken. He is coming back I thought and added my mother's mantra: 'Thank God. Thank God. Thank God. Thank God!'

Soon after that he said, 'What do you think of me being a songwriter?'

Christine and I heard his first song at Rockfield. He sang it 'A cappella' as there was no music yet but it was called 'I love my life' and the words were radiantly happy. He had found a path.

History repeated itself. I had always wondered why my mother had snapped people's heads off when they asked her, 'Suh, is Judy, ahhhm, still doing the painting?'

'Yes, that's what painters do you know, they paint.'

Now it was my turn.

'Aahmmm, suh, what's Alexei doing with himself?'

'He is writing songs and singing them. He is a songwriter.'

Silently, I would do a slow count, 'one-two-three-four' and then, 'Well, as long as he's happy.'

'Mom they speak to me, with their eyes so full of pity. It must be so hard they say and I have to turn away so they don't see my smile because I love what I'm doing so much!'

Because I believe that any endeavor that follows one's bliss has a good chance of succeeding, I did not hesitate to give it my support. Dave's horror though could not be expressed. He had started saving for Alexei's education from the day he was born and saw the money as wasted. How could he not be disappointed at the turn of events? With justification he cut off all assistance but in the face of Alexei's subsequent survival, for which a stint in India believe me was a good preparation, he softened enough to come to a performance a few years later.

A man of few words, as he was, but always genuine, he pronounced it, 'Tremendous!'

It was Christmas at Rockfield and significantly, his father was visiting from America, when Sabrina was brought to join us for the weekend. She was calm and pleasant without being over friendly, what we called in the '60s, 'cool' and this attractive manner was matched by a unique beauty – an hour glass figure and long, honey-coloured hair. When they were leaving she said, 'Thank you Joodie, it's a long time I have not been in a family.' His father and I liked her very much.

Alexei was spending a lot of time in Negril, which is a favourite haunt of Italians in Jamaica and where Sabrina lived. I did not see her again until about a year later when Alexei invited me to join them for lunch and said, 'Mom, I've asked Sabrina to marry me.'

I got up from my chair and embraced him, moved by his trust in life at twenty-seven years old. Afterwards I said to him, 'Darling, most men have no idea how to choose a woman, but it would surprise you how well we women size each other up. This is a very intelligent choice. This is a clean woman. She looks you right in the eye. No sneakiness. She will never be negative, never pull you down. Best of all she laughs. If the roof falls in or they cut off the water she will laugh and that laughter will lighten life when it gets heavy.'

Her first comment to me when I was told at that lunch that they were getting married was.

'I don't want any trouble with you Joodie.'

'Me neither, Darling, me neither.'

We all know that life can go wrong in a minute, it's so fragile and so impossible to predict but at time of writing, when I look into my son's face, I see a happy man.

7

Jimmy

Play fool fe ketch wise

Alexei was four when I met Jimmy. I was twenty nine years old and my painting life was established. Although I felt destined and that painting had chosen me, not the other way around, I had many doubts, because I was not filled with a mad passion to paint in a frenzy all night. Nor did I ever feel like cutting off an ear or anything like that.

I had run from marriage but not from men. I learned to walk into parties alone, looking a lot more confident than I felt. I liked men a lot but I knew something was missing. In other words, the earth hadn't moved yet.

The quest to find the one who would make it move was fun and there were lots of contenders. On second thoughts maybe the word 'quest' dignifies an activity that would be better described as going 'hog wild' for a while. The point is that I called the shots. I picked and discarded and prided myself on being as cool about it as any man. Mostly I picked foreigners though because although I found Jamaican men attractive I had a problem with them.

Yu mean, they had a problem with you.

Maybe it was because during the teenage years, when boys and girls learn to relate to each other, I was away in Scotland. I had not learned the bantering way that men and women speak to each other on the island.

A typical conversation would go like this: 'Aren't you the MacMillan girl?'

'Errrr … yes.'

'Suh, what's the story?'

I would be left dumbfounded and puzzled by the belligerent tone and lurch off as quickly as my high-heeled shoes would allow.

Painting whole exhibitions of nudes, which seemed perfectly normal to me, was also misunderstood in a prudish society. After all, we all know what lies on the underside of prudishness. These nudes had received a lot of publicity in the press, so invariably at cocktail parties a man would sidle up to me and say: 'Heh heh heh, yu want to paint me naked?'

'Sure.'

'How much would it cost?'

'Nothing. I'll pay you.'

I was spending a lot of time with my amusing mentor and soul mate, Colin Garland, a brilliant surrealist painter. But if you become friends with a gay man in no time at all you will know thirty. After all the fun and giggles are over, it can get boring for a girl.

When the student is ready, the master appears.

Jimmy was the 'likkle' brother of friends and had just come back to the island from a course in hotel management in Germany. I met him on his parent's verandah where the whole family was sitting one afternoon when I dropped in for a visit.

I tried not to look at the ridiculous person across from me who went into an exaggerated performance as soon as he saw me. It was a lip licking, eye-ogling, forward-leaning, writhing and squirming burlesque. This pantomime strongly suggested that, despite the polite conversation going on around us, he would soon throw me down on the tiles and do it right there in front of everybody.

'Oh my God. What an idiot.'

How could my friends who I thought were so smart have such a cretinous younger brother?

But wait. Ah you de fool. Him a play fool fe catch wise

A few days later there was a knock on my studio door and he was standing on the doorstep. He looked as if he just stepped out of the shower, I thought, as I listened to his request. He had come to commission me to do a portrait of himself nude for a girl in London.

How much would it cost?

'A thousand dollars.'

That was a huge sum in those days and I chose it in order to end this rubbish right away. He didn't blink though and agreed to the fee. He said with a straight face that he particularly wanted his 'cock' painted in great detail – veins, highlights, hairs and everything. Could I do that?

'Oh yes', I assured him, with a straight face.

'When can we start?'

'Right away. Take off your clothes.'

That usually was the end of that but he simply took them off.

Taken aback by this move and hoisted on my own petard, I reached for a large canvas and started to squeeze paint on to my palette. Peeking over I saw that he was lying flat on the small bed in the studio with his arms folded across his chest. He was looking at me, very much the busy painter, squeezing paint and pouring fresh turpentine, with an inscrutable look on his face.

'That's not a very good pose, better sit up over here on this sofa.'

I started the painting and the whole time he talked to me in a soft voice all about women. He said the more beautiful they were the more lonely because most men did not understand them. Utterly ridiculous, I thought, and wished he would be quiet. But the painting was going well. When it was at a good stage to stop I finished and made an appointment for the next sitting. When he left I was talking to a painter friend of mine on the phone.

'You'll never guess what happened today, one of those little Kingston studs came in here and commissioned a nude portrait. What do you think I should do with him?'

'I think you should jump on him!'

In spite of myself I was intrigued because a strange thing had happened. Although I had painted many men nude and many of them had good bodies, simply the sight of the naked male body did not excite me. A photograph of a naked female body in a sleazy magazine could excite me more because I would imagine the effect on a man. But I had never before been seduced visually by the sheer appearance of a man. His body was the most spectacular I'd ever seen. It was perfect.

When he came back for the second sitting, the idea that my friend had unwittingly planted in my mind had taken hold but I had no idea in this world how to go about it. So I just painted away. He told me he was nineteen and he seemed as innocent as a child with his soft voice, perfect body and gigantic dark penis – that stayed erect from the start of the sitting right through to the end.

This phenomenon was something I was quite accustomed to ignoring in my line of work.

When I was living on Hope Road and Bap the goat herder was our neighbour, I asked him one morning over the fence to pose for me. He thought for awhile and said, 'There is oney one 'ooman I evah do dat fah … and ar name was Edna Manley.'

In truth, he looked exactly like that statue of Bogle that she did – a short, tough little man – and now I know where she got the idea for the huge machete that he holds down the front of his body.

'Oh good, well you remember what you did for Edna, I want you to do the same for me.'

'Oney trouble is I am a man that sometime get hard.'

'Not to worry, can't stay up all the time!'

How very wrong I was.

When we got to the studio and Bap stripped, I saw that he was afflicted with a penis that looked like a prize-winning plantain. He sat down on the edge of a chair with his pelvis thrust forward and it cascaded down and almost touched the floor. My mind raced as to how to compose the painting with this totally out of proportion element so I asked him to stand. In this new stance, I took some artistic license and made it a little shorter so as to have a bit of white background below it to balance the composition. That resolved I began to paint.

He talked continuously as I recall about 'young gal' and how 'dem hot' and so on but I had learned to concentrate totally on my work and to phase out annoying distractions. I entered that painting for a competition of Jamaican paintings going to Canada. I thought it would refute the ideas that I was reading about at the time of 'the myth' of the black penis. No myth I'm afraid but it was rejected from the selection. Although it had only been at The Institute of Jamaica – a dusty, seldom visited place – for a few days before it was rejected, everyone in Kingston seemed to have heard about it. My friend Georgie, Lady Colin Campbell, whom I also painted nude at that time asked when she saw it, 'Judy Ann, do you mean to tell me that you had this in your studio and did not try it out?'

'My dear Georgie, I haven't the remotest interest in pain.'

Dudley Guillermo Malcolm MacMillan. My father as a young man.

My favourite picture of my parents, Vida Juanita Rose & Dudley Guilermo Malcom MacMillan, in the 1940s.

My parent's wedding outside Coke Chapel, Kingston1944. From the left: my mother's mother; Hilda Garcia Fullerton; best man, Abe Issa; the bride and groom; my mother's father, Sydney Leopold Fullerton and my father's mother, Helen MacMillan.

At West Avenue, with my brother Robert and our pony, Dandy.

My mother in the garden at West Avenue.

My father with Abe Issa & Errol Flynn.

The Colony Club.

A party for Nat King Cole and his wife at West Avenue. Guests include: Mr & Mrs Nat King Cole; Mr & Mrs Ferdie Martin; Mr & Mrs Barry Rose; Miss Vida Menzies; Miss Hazel Lopez; Baronness Barovier de Riel; Mr & Mrs Michael Zaidie; Mr & Mrs Granville DaCosta; Sir Herbert MacDonald.

West Avenue in Constant Spring – the Art Deco house that was my childhood home.

With Christine and Rosemary Lai Fook in Trafalgar Square, London.

At sixteen, when I went to art school in Dundee.

Mummy in the 1960s.

My first exhibition with Sir Phillip Sherlock & Edna Manley who opened the show.

At my wedding to David Julian Russell, St Andrew Parish Churuch, Kingson, April 1969.

With my new born son, David Alexander Russell, Ohio, February 1970. I always called him Alexei.

My father with his first grandson.

In London, with John Johnstone, Alexei and Mummy in the 1970s.

Alexei, aged five, and me. These were my happiest years.

I was interested in Jimmy though, so at the break I sat beside him on the sofa and started showing him a book, the only one in the studio, which was 'The Human Figure in Motion' by Eadweard Muybridge. He said afterwards that he didn't know how he kept from laughing because he knew exactly what I was doing. I have always rated him highly for figuring me out and coming up with the ideal way to get my undivided attention.

The actual act was a cataclysmic ravishment of such ferocity that I was terrified at what I had done. Do not think it was enjoyable. It was not. I was so scared that all I thought about was my safety because he was obviously insane. The shocking change from sweet little lamb to raging gorilla was schizophrenic. Think of the power mower going over the grass or the Rape of the Sabine women or Alexander sacking Rome and you've got it – conquest pure and simple.

Afterwards, he ordered me to get his shoes and put them on. There was a movie at the time called *Swept Away* with just such a scene but he didn't go to movies and hadn't seen it. I did exactly as he said because I was sure that I was dealing with a lunatic and thought, Judy Ann, you have made some mistakes in your life but this one takes the cake. Just do exactly what he says, I advised myself get him out the door and then you don't ever have to see him again.

Now you may well wonder how come it did happen again and I truly do not know. I was certainly in a new terrain. I was conquered by a superior force and I surrendered. Thus began my erotic exploration of the wilder shores of love. It turned out that he was twenty-five and that we were distantly related.

'Cousin boil good soup.'

Needless to say I was never paid for the painting. When it was exhibited for sale at my next show, at which all the other models were present, I was asked where he was and I said, 'Probably can't find a thing to wear.'

When it was exhibited in New York a woman came up to me and asked me for his phone number.

There was a strong mystique about his family. They were famously wild. My mother said that when she was young her sisters used to sit around the kitchen table and talk about what his uncles were doing up the road in Vineyard Town.

He was proud of the family legend and it was certainly interesting because it was deeply woven into the history of the island. They had arrived at the time of Cromwell and owned just about every property in the centre of the island at an earlier time.

Jimmy's rural ancestors had taken very seriously the Biblical command to go forth and multiply. There were thousands of illegitimate relatives all over the countryside with a striking resemblance to him around the lips and eyebrows.

We, never in the years we were together, went on a conventional date. On the first 'date' with him he drove over the mountains from Kingston to the coast and built a bonfire on a magnificent stretch of beach. When evening came and I was thinking that was nice but it's time to go home now, he said, 'Let's go and get Alexei and sleep here tonight.'

'What? Are you insane?'

We drove all the way back to my little house in Kingston where he picked up a few utensils from the kitchen. He threw a blanket in the car, a couple of oil lanterns along with Alexei and his best friend who lived in a neighbouring house.

Then we drove all the way back to the bushy area behind that beach and stopped at a little teepee-shaped hut made of coconut fronds that are sometimes put up by cattle herders for shelter. As he entered the area he explained to a man on the side of the path, 'We are going to sleep here tonight, so if you see us, don't be alarmed.'

Later I learned, when painting landscapes, that the bush was divided into 'querencias' with unmarked boundaries. Only the people who lived there knew the perimeter. I would overhear quarrels sometimes with bellowed orders to outsiders who had crossed that invisible line.

'Ah seh, come out, come out of we area.'

Informing the man that we were in his territory was the right thing to do. Then he made a little camp by spreading the brightly coloured blanket inside the hut and lighting the lanterns. It was such an adventure that I thought the children were going to vaporise with delight. Before dawn, I was awakened by a loud chomping sound right at my ear.

'Jimmy, I think a cow is eating down our house.'

It was a feeling of total freedom to find myself on that beach at dawn. A tension pain that I had in my neck was gone and when I remarked on that he said, 'Miss Mac you just need a little rough life.'

He called me 'Miss Mac' because that's what we called our cleaning lady at my father's cinema where my studio was located. It was to take me down a peg. The name stuck and I was Miss Mac to most of our friends in those years.

Jimmy had no interest in my social life so that continued but with the dessert waiting at home. He adored hiding in a cupboard or under the bed because a favourite fantasy was that he was the gardener having it off with the mistress of the house on the sly.

Early on, when our affair was still secret, I was going out to the theatre one evening with Colin, the painter. Jimmy was concealed in my clothes closet while Colin walked around the whole small house chatting to Alexei until I finished dressing.

'Ok lets go.'

I walked out leaving the front door open. Colin said, 'Are you going out leaving Alexei alone in the house?'

'Have you ever seen me leave Alexei alone in the house? Of course not.'

As I was reversing the car out of the car park, 'But Judy, who is with Alexei?'

'The babysitter.'

Still later as the curtain was parting at the theatre, 'Judy, where was the babysitter?'

'The babysitter was in the closet.'

During this same period, an American came by the townhouse early one evening. He had been given my name by a mutual friend as someone to make contact with when in Jamaica. After a chat he invited me to dinner and I accepted so he went out to the car park to tell his waiting taxi to go. Jimmy crossed his path skipping down in the opposite direction to my house. I put my index finger up to my lips and without words he slipped upstairs and hopped into my bed to watch me dress to go out with another man.

The whole operation had to be conducted in silence of course. I would take out a dress and he would shake his head violently. Or I would select another and he would nod with approval. One pair of shoes was rejected – a sexier pair passed the test. When I was dressed, made up and combed to his complete satisfaction, as I kissed him goodbye, he whispered,

'My girl must look hot.'

We had something important in common. We were both misfits. Like me, he perched on the edge of many groups. He would even fly in for a while but we didn't really belong in groups. We didn't drink and he detested drugs. In fact was repelled by even the smell of ganja, so without the shared use of drugs and alcohol many erstwhile friends were lost without regret. I was discovering with him an invaluable rural etiquette as he showed me how to be safe in the wild natural heart of the country. And as if that wasn't enough, I would never have seen Rockfield without him.

My parents typically were divided. My mother was vociferously in mourning for her docile daughter. While my father, whose code would not allow him to interfere with anyone's love life, even mine, restricted himself to sarcasm. He could not take seriously any man who was not at his desk at nine o'clock on Monday morning. But for a man who would not have a drink and whose briefcase accidentally opened to reveal a comic book and a tooth brush, well, he had no words at all for that.

Jimmy was in complete sympathy with my father's view. He said that if he had a daughter like me who was carrying on with a man like him that he wouldn't like it either.

'Miss Mac, all he sees when he looks at me is wild hog inna him coco.'

The wild hog kept fit by placing his feet on a chair and doing fifty push ups at what looked like a comfortable, leisurely pace, clapping between each one. Hardly a man's man, the wild hog thought that his fellow men were stupid, that women were of superior intelligence. He was never happier than when he was the only man included on a weekend with a huge crowd of women. The wild hog adored women: of all ages; all colours; all races and in return for that rarest of traits, women adored him right back.

Ah ram goat dat!

The archetypal myth that rules Jamaica is 'the trickster'. Our version of the trickster is called Anansi, a spider hero whose achievements are not of heroic exploits but of outsmarting his opponents. Traveling through the countryside with Jimmy was like being with Anansi himself, albeit a Rabelaisian version.

Holding obscenely onto his 'pants front' (groin) he would suddenly declare: 'Now some men have buddy, some have willie, some have cockie but DIS is HOOD.'

Or in tourist guide mode to visiting foreigners, 'Listen, don't fall asleep under a paw paw tree. You will lose yu nature. On the other hand, beat yu cock against de trunk of the paw paw tree if yu want to get a big cock.'

Certainly I never met before or since a man with a more unbridled relish for his own genitalia than Jimmy.

The subject matter for painting comes from choices that are so deeply subjective, that it is hard even for the painter to explain but I know that my landscape painting which started as secondary in importance to my figures took precedence because of this new visual source.

A dutiful daughter, I had never before been irresponsible, I had never laughed until I was weak or headed into the wilderness without money, food, accommodation or gas in the car. I was in a new reality of heart stopping beauty far from the Jamaica of hotels and waiters: swimming in icy rivers with pale green water; making love in caves behind waterfalls; eating fruit just cut from the tree; sleeping on cliff tops with the sound of the sea crashing below us while he talked all night to fishermen whose faces were lit up by kerosene lanterns. That heightened state with every sense alive included the anguish of imminent loss. The island was transformed by the worse political upheaval that it had ever known and there was an exodus from Jamaica along with enormous tension, melodrama and genuine fear. This was the 1970s when Michael Manley's Peoples National Party (PNP) captured the votes of the poorest level in the society by simply offering them power. 'Power' was a potent propaganda word, which was stronger than the Opposition's – the Jamaica Labour Party (JLP) – 'freedom' because the poor are already free.

I was also painting portraits of the street people on a daily basis. The studio was always full of models. Often Nana, a beggar who was a ferocious devotee of the PNP, would stop by for a 'likkle' modeling work. Every time she came, I would ask her to say 'power' for me and happy to be asked she would go into her performance. She would plant one foot to steady her and shake her entire body up from this pivotal point with the arms rising and shaking to triumphant rays above her head and scream, 'P-O-W-A-H-H-H!'

'Wi nuh want nuh weevil flowah, wi want POWAH!' (Weevil flour referred to a shipment of bad flour that came into the island and the opposition party, the JLP was blamed for it.)

Sex and politics are a potent enough mix but apart from our sexual chemistry, Jimmy loved Alexei and he knew just how to disarm his childish jealousy. He never tried to be an authority figure, which would have usurped his absent father's role, playing with him instead as a brother. He certainly passed on some of his expertise with, that different species, girls. When Alexei, aged eight, was invited to a birthday party telling me of the invitation at the last minute much too late to get a present for the birthday girl, Jimmy saved the day by saying, 'Look Sport, pick a flower and walk right up and give it to her. She will like it better than all the presents that she gets.'

We watched Alexei with his back straight march into the house holding his flower and Jimmy said, 'Proud of this young cock coming up.'

His views on my other love, painting challenged me. For example, on the subject of commissions which I hated doing he said.

'Miss Mac, you think if you are not painting ole negar lying on a bed or sitting on a chair it's not art. A real artist suppose to be able to paint anything anyone give them to paint, from a bird in flight to a hawse or a cow, anything. You think it's "pressure" to please the client. Pressure? You don't know what pressure is. The old painters that you love, they painted for the King, that was pressure. If he didn't like the picture they didn't just lose de wuk, they did lose dem *head*. An you know what else, Miss Mac? That's what made them *good*.'

I squirmed because there was an element of truth in this earthy wisdom.

My studio was in a big detached building at the back of my father's advertising agency and the location was convenient for my growing cast of players. On one occasion, a group of workmen were building on a site next to the studio. Every day as I passed one of them would chant, 'Babylon mus fah-all,' like a sweet, soft refrain in a song. This practice of singing an insult or prediction of doom that obliquely refers to you – but that you are not supposed to hear – is classic insider communication in Jamaica. Playing my role meant ignoring it so as to appear fooled.

One lunchtime, the singer appeared in the doorway of the studio and elaborately draping his lanky body on the door said,

'Can you advance me a lunch money?'

'Sure, but can you answer one question? What's going to happen when Babylon falls, if Zion feeds off Babylon?'

'Ah like to reason with you.'

His delighted smile lit up his whole face. His unmasked face was radiant. We became friends, or allies anyway, for a while and he posed for a portrait. I called it *Cawchee Blow* because at the same time every day he would whisper in the still silence of the studio, 'Cawchee blow' and finally taught me to hear a faint horn from as far away as the wharf at the bottom of Kingston which signals the end of a work shift. It comes from slavery days when the horn that was blown was a conch shell. I would know that it would soon be time to get Alexei from school.

My models would overlap in the studio and there would be occasionally a clash of religions, or religious one-upmanship. The most memorable incident was when a young Rasta and a very old lady, Miss Myers, were there together one day.

The Rasta was as usual going on and on about Ethiopia's Haile Selassie who the Rastas believe to be God. Miss Myers dozed and woke intermittently as the old sometimes do. I drew in silence. At one point in the Rasta's 'argument' he said that Haile Selassie was Christ in the Second Advent, in other words, the promised Second coming of Christ had already taken place.

Miss Myers snapped awake with a question.

'Do you mean to tell me that dis Haile Selassie is the same Lord Jesus Christ who did die on de cross far us all?'

'Yes … de very same.'

'Who is his madda?'

'What?'

'I believe dat Christ on de cross did make a reference to his madder so who is dis Haile Selassie's madder?'

The Rasta stormed out muttering and very annoyed and I said to Miss Myers, 'You raised a serious theological point Miss Myers and it's the first time I've seen a Rasta stumped.'

From memory, I painted the scores of 'mad people' who multiplied in the streets at that time. They were visually magnificent beings who, like lizards, could be seen in the exact same places every day. Although there was sympathy in my heart for them, the paintings were more concerned with their haunting aesthetic. I watched them cruise each other when they passed in the street. One with a blonde, blue-eyed doll wrapped around her middle another with an endless scarf blowing behind him, made of garbage bags tied together, like Isadora Duncan.

It was 1977 the year of 'the two sevens meeting' and a dire prediction was in the air about blood flowing in Swallowfield which was quite near to where I lived. I used to drive up in the hills to avoid the coast road on my way to Duncans for week-ends. Often I would have friends with me and would always stop at the highest point to look at a broad valley above St Ann's Bay, to share the panoramic view and often I would say, 'This is my dream in life, to wake every morning and look at this valley.'

Then I would hop back in the car and go on with my life and forget it. I certainly did not remember it the day that Jimmy asked me to come to St Ann to look for a property for a client. I may have forgotten to mention that real estate was his work but he never seemed to be doing all that much work. There was nothing I liked more than exploring so I agreed. We saw five very special houses that day. The first one had that lovely Georgian shape and big sash windows.

'Do you like it?'

'Like it? I love it. I'd live there tomorrow.'

In the afternoon he turned up an overgrown track. At the top of the steep, deeply rutted track was the most breathtaking view I'd ever seen and a magical deserted house, which I felt sure I'd seen before in another life. The electrifying sensation of déjà vu gave me goose bumps.

We walked around the desolate, abandoned place. It was smothered by weeds, crushed by vines and haunted by dup-pies but to me it was utterly compelling.

At the back was a little cottage with a stone foundation: the walls looked eighteenth century with a quirky Victorian addition on the top. Between the house and the outbuildings at the back were extensive barbecues; these are terraces, which were once used for drying pimento and also as catchments for rainwater.

'You know what would be nice Jimmy, to get this little place and fix it up and use it on weekends.'

I was thinking of the perfect place to paint the landscapes without having to drive long distances and stop before I wanted to. He was looking at the large main house in front when he said, 'You know what would be even nicer, Miss Mac? To get that house.'

The track that led to Rockfield had another veering off it, which led to an adjacent hill. He drove over there next. The road ended at a charming well-kept house and he opened the gate and drove in. He was going to enquire if the abandoned house next door was for sale. I heard my mother's voice when anyone was intrepid enough to ask if the house at West Avenue was for sale.

'What gave you the impression that the house was for sale? Did you see a 'For Sale' sign anywhere?'

'Oh God Jimmy man, I hate when you do this.'

A dear little old lady wearing a cardigan with a little scatter pin seemed absolutely delighted to see us. She had obviously 'tidied for the afternoon' and was accepting visitors. She was sitting on the verandah with her little dog.

Indeed, the house next door was for sale as were so many in the '70s. It belonged to her sister-in-law and was in the hands of a real estate company called C.D. Alexander in Kingston. Her sister-in-law had lived there until about a year or so ago but was now at Eden Bower, which was a small boarding house for the aged in Ocho Rios.

It was six o'clock and we had no gas in the car because in the wartime conditions of the times there were gas restrictions. In spite of that, Jimmy headed for Ocho Rios immediately with me yelling at him for being a maniac the whole way. Ocho Rios was about forty minutes away but mostly downhill and he was adept at coasting to save gas so we free-wheeled hair-raisingly most of the way.

In the pitch dark I heard him banging on the door and this frail little old lady tremulously answering his barrage of questions without opening the door.

'Ahhhhmm Miss Cotter, Rockfield, tell me something, is it for sale?'

'How much do you want for the place?'

'Oh dear me, it's in the hands of C.D. Alexander you see?'

He hopped back in the car and don't ask me how he got us back to Kingston.

I was possessed by Rockfield and couldn't get it out of my mind but I really wasn't thinking of owning it myself when he suggested that I buy it.

'But I can't afford to buy a house.'

'Miss Mac, you have no ambition.'

He wrote to C.D. Alexander and offered forty thousand dollars. There was no response. In a month's time he offered thirty thousand dollars. Still, there was no response.

Now that the idea has taken root in my mind and he had convinced me that I could do it, I went to my father for advice. He drove out with us to see the place. I have photographs of that day and the look on my father's face is so grave that I smile to myself now. Rockfield was his idea of a nightmare on the face of the earth. By this time we had permission to go inside. I adored it and didn't see the missing floorboards or ceiling panels. I only saw the beautiful moulding, the fireplaces, the high ceilings and the sash windows. He only saw a derelict house on a barren hill covered in scrappy weeds and grass lice, with rain water tanks full of froggy water, no telephone and no clients.

He said, 'Darling this is a disastrous idea. I wouldn't touch this with a ten-foot pole. This will bleed you of money. Besides you are a young woman, what are you going to do? Sit on a verandah up here and rock?'

'I'm going to paint landscapes for the rest of my life and sell them.'

Jimmy wrote to the estate agent again and this time offered twenty-five thousand dollars.'

'Just keep cool, Miss Mac. I'm going to get the house for you for fifteen thousand dollars.

My nerves cracked. My father said, 'Don't be clever, Judy. If you want the place, go to the old lady, tell her exactly how much money you have and ask her to sell it to you.'

Miss Cotter was in Kingston having her cataracts removed and she couldn't see me as I spoke.

'Miss Cotter, I don't have much money. Twenty thousand dollars. The place is worth much more but this is all I have. I love Rockfield. It's exactly like finding a good home for a dog. I will love the place as much as your family did.'

'You know, my father used to walk around the place with a paint pot in his hand, touching it up.'

'I can see how well it was cared for.'

'All my life people have been telling me to cut down that big thatch palm that is so near to the house.'

'Don't worry I won't touch that palm. I love it too.'

Finally the company responded to say that if we did not 'pay down' in two days, after all that time, we would lose the house. I went to my mother and we drove to St Ann.

'Well darling,' she said ' you have to have it. I don't think it's the best view I've seen in Jamaica. I think it's the best view I've seen in the world. If you don't get it we will have to put you in a sanatorium for the rest of your life and throw away the key.'

I had two thousand dollars in the bank, the proceeds from sales of my sets of prints. But I had Daddy's real estate mantra in my mind, 'First, pay down. That stops anyone else from getting it. Then figure out how you are going to pay for it.'

So I paid down my two thousand dollars. When my father came back from his trip I went to see him in his office. It was the very first time I had not taken his advice.

'Serious ting.'

'Well, I've defied you. I've paid down on Rockfield. I thought about what you said, about it being impractical. Right now I am living in a practical town house, taking my son to school, doing everything that I'm supposed to do but the truth is, I am not a practical person. Am I to live as a fraud for the rest of my life?'

His secretary told me that when I left the office he laughed and admitted to her that he was glad I had bought it. I can see him now, his tongue in his cheek, with slow tears of amusement rolling out of the corners of his eyes.

It was mine but it was being ransacked fast. There was not one stick of furniture in the house only a broken majolica vase but on my next visit I found all the bathtubs and basins out on the lawn just waiting for a truck to move them and a huge pile of books had been dumped on the grass. They were ruined in the rain. The ancient water heater was gone and someone had started ripping out the wiring.

Jimmy and I drove down to Eden Bower again where Miss Cotter, her eye operation in Kingston over, had returned. There was a group of visitors sitting on the verandah there when I went straight into my story.

'Miss Cotter, if I don't get possession now, there won't be any point getting it at all.'

I described what was going on at the house.

'Oh dear me and I have hired a man to watch over the place you know.'

'But it's obviously him doing it!'

'What a scamp, eh?'

One of her visitors, an old gentleman with white hair had been quietly listening to my impassioned report. He now spoke.

'Miss MacMillan allow me to introduce myself, my name is Frank Roxborough. I am brother-in-law to Miss Cotter and I live in the area. I will go to Rockfield tomorrow and I will secure the house. I will take your bathtubs and washbasins to Anandale where you can collect them at your convenience. Go over to Winefield, the house on the property next door to Rockfield, and present yourself to Eddie Hairs. Tell him that I sent you. He will take care of you.'

I thanked this great gentleman and did exactly as he said.

Respect. Respect due. Maximum respect

Next I went to a lawyer called Hurley Whitehorne in Ocho Rios.

'Hello. I'm Judy MacMillan.'

He gave me a blank stare.

'I'm the person who brought Rockfield.'

His blank stare continued.

'Aren't you Miss Cotter's lawyer?'

'No, I am Mrs Cotter's lawyer.'

She was the lady at the house next door, in the cardigan with the dog.

'Please may I make a call to Miss Cotter from here?'

I called Miss Cotter and asked if she would like me to retain Hurley Whitehorne to be her lawyer.

'Veddy good of you.'

The remaining payments would be spread over seven years.

Jimmy and I would go down sometimes to spend a day at the house. Between the flowerbeds in the formal garden was hideous white gravel and the first thing that I wanted to do was take that up and plant grass. We did it ourselves without a wheelbarrow by piling up the stones into a box with two poles attached that Jimmy made and dumping them over the precipice at the front. The beds were lined with old grey conch shells. I kept those. On the way back into town, all covered in scrapes as I was, I would cry a little with happiness: that's always a sure sign that you are doing the right thing.

The first night we spent in our huge dolly house was hardly romantic because Jimmy, who hadn't lived at the movies as I had when I was growing up, had a way of keeping Hollywood-style romance at bay. While I was upstairs making a cosy nest with sheets and pillows for our mattress on the floor, he was downstairs banging loudly with a hammer. He booby-trapped the whole house by placing, on top of doorways, things that would collapse on intruding heads if anyone tried to push the door. His loud progress through the house ended at the upstairs bedroom.

He totally ignored my little celebratory picnic basket with some cold roasted chicken and a bottle of wine and had started to nail the door of the bedroom shut behind him when I protested.

'Oh God, Jimmy man, stop ruining that lovely door. This is so, so unromantic.'

'It won't be too romantic if somebody comes up here and chops us up, Miss Mac.'

A long time after that first evening, I suddenly remembered about my dream in life being to wake up every morning and see that valley.

It was the same valley.

8

Rockfield

Young bud nuh know storm

The first painting I did at Rockfield was a panoramic view from the front. On the left was the little bay that Christopher Columbus first sailed into when he discovered Jamaica in 1494. Beside the bay a small part of the flat sugar lands of Richmond Llandovery Estate was visible. All my landscapes at that time were inspired by the nineteenth century lithographs by the itinerant topographers James Hakewell and James Kidd. The views around Rockfield looked exactly like them. The view from that tiny bay resembled an 's' lying on its side, which may well have inspired Columbus's famous description, 'the fairest isle that eyes have beheld.'

During the course of the painting the valley filled up with the saffron-coloured blossoms of the Immortelle trees and I put them in. I worked for several months on that painting and gave it to my father.

'Jimmy will you please leave me alone to paint? Look at the lengths, Dear God, I have gone to, to just get a chance to paint. I beg you. I AM BEGGING YOU leave me AH-LONE!'

And he would happily drive down to the coast to hunt 'tourist chicks' all day long, which was his favourite sport anyway.

The first time that I painted for nine hours without a break in concentration was one of the most ecstatic days of my life. I called the painting *Nine Hours in St Ann* and never touched it again. I had an unbroken circle of beauty and my life wasn't going to be long enough to do it all. Was it a good painting? I didn't know and I didn't care. The painting itself was a pale souvenir of an experience that had become its own reason for being.

The house itself was rough. There was no kitchen, not even a sink. I would cook on a coal-stove which I learned the hard way you can't ever turn down. I was using dry wood to make the fire so everything had a smoked tandoori flavour. One day I was squatting under one of the huge water tanks to wash up dishes with Mr Mucho Macho standing over me watching.

'Boy yu father should see this ... what I've brought you to.'

'The difference between you and my father my dear, is that he would only have to see this once and he would buy me a sink: but you are prepared to see this for the rest of your life.'

He bought me a little secondhand sink and 'cotched' it up in our makeshift kitchen. It emptied right outside in a garden bed. So with a coal stove, a Styrofoam cooler with a block of ice that I bought from a lady on the main road for a fridge, we were able to entertain and had lunch parties and played in our doll's house.

Overnight guests got a mattress on the floor, a kerosene lantern for light and a machete to keep under their mattress for security. We would lie flat on the barbeques and marvel at the stars; the rooms would fill up with peenie wallies – thousands of them. I would fall asleep to a dance of tiny lights above me. The water – dipped up in buckets from the water tank – was cold and the house full of freezing drafts that reminded me of Scotland, as did the layers of hilly pastures stretching back each lined in mist.

The caress of the mountain breezes felt wonderful on my skin after the heat of Kingston. The sunset every single evening was an event not to be missed, we would race up the hill to get there in time for it. Sparrow hawks circled in the evening sky hunting, their wings flashed red gold as they plummeted. It was pitch black on starless nights and silent, except for a philharmonic orchestra of a billion tiny creatures. Little cruise ships, lit up like rhinestones, floated past at an improbable height.

The house was just a fragile shell with hardly any separation from nature. It wasn't just a house to me. It was a sort of rapture.

Jimmy built a tree house for Alexei and we explored the whole area finding rivers, ponds, waterfalls, huge stands of bamboo, wild orchids and sour wild fruit.

In the morning, which is still my favourite time, the Blue Mountains can be seen way in the distance. They are a clean, flat blue and look as if a child drew them but by midmorning they disappear in the haze. The view was very difficult to paint because there was hardly any foreground. It was all distance air and space. At the foot of the track about a mile or so down was the main road. There was one, tiny shop owned by Miss Ruby and I decided that anything I could not get in Miss Ruby's shop I could probably do without. She had never sold a whole pack of cigarettes. People bought a couple or even six but not a whole pack.

I found all the country characters enchanting in my early euphoria. Mas Joe, a cow penner, was in my life from the start and eventually kept his cows on the land. I would sing out like Mary Poppins in my paint stained clothes: 'Good morning Mas Joe, isn't it a lovely day?'

'Every day is a lovely day miss.'

Dealing with employees was very different to what I was used to with my progressive town ways. I learned the rural lore from Jimmy who would say to a man from the village – a tall older man called Mr Grant – who we hired sporadically to help in the weed-filled garden.

'Do me a favour, just have the floors polished for me before we come back next week.'

Driving off my eyes popping I would say, 'But how do you expect him to do that? There isn't a mop or a broom or polish or anything?'

'Jus relax, nuh.'

We would return and find the dark mahogany floors like glass. Solondine is a wild bush with juicy stalks. They crush the stalks and rub the juices into the wood and then burnish them with a hard dry coconut brush, which is more like a stone than a brush. To do a whole house like that I thought horribly hard and it made me feel uncomfortable and guilty.

The first New Year after we got the house, this same Mr Grant, asked if he could use the house to have a family reunion. His family would be coming from near and far for the Christmas holidays, even as far away as the legendary St Mary where everyone's relatives seemed to live. Rockfield was empty, unfurnished and without electric light yet, as we had not had the wiring checked. It seemed mean to say 'no', but I felt a little uneasy so I made one weak stipulation that right after New Year's Eve every body was to leave.

Driving down the hill Jimmy and I agreed that we had made a mistake and that if we had not been caught off guard it would have been nice to spend New Year's Eve there ourselves. Mistake? It was a disaster. Fifteen days after the deadline I drove down to Rockfield with … my mother.

Yes Lawd!

At the entrance to the track I said, 'Now Mummy, if you see any extraneous people at the house please say nothing, you know you and I deal with things in different ways.'

As we drove in the first thing that struck us was a tall locks man standing on the verandah. I felt my mother stiffen silently beside me. When we got out of the car Mr Grant came out to greet us with a large group of little yapping dogs who circled my feet.

'Oh! Who brought all these little dogs here?'

'I did.'

'But, but, Mr Grant I don't like these little dogs at all.'

'I like dem dough.'

Um Hmmmm ... Man a yard!

We walked into the house and found it furnished. Every room was crammed with furniture, dressing tables, huge wardrobes and beds. Curtains were hung in all the windows. Mr Grant showed us visitors around proudly and flicked on a light switch to show off that he had connected the electricity as well.

Stifling a scream I proceeded to the back. In our temporary kitchen there was a table and a little old man was sitting at it dressed, as we say, 'to puss back foot' in a three-piece church suit. He looked up and saw my mother in her white slacks, straw hat and jewellery and said audibly to himself, 'What bad luck.'

Outside on the barbeques was a village scene It was genre painting by a tropical Bruegel: with children; women at coal stoves roasting yams; washing clothes in pans; sheets drying on clotheslines and more dogs.

Come si mi an come live wid mi is two different tings

My mind was racing. Mr Grant looked down on me as if he were contemplating an ant.

'Mummy, lets go!'

I noticed in passing that a lychee tree I had asked him

to plant was dead. In the car, not surprisingly, my mother exploded. I don't know how she didn't have an embolism but I was thankful that at the house she had not said one word.

'WHAT ARE YOU GOING TO DO NOW, YOU LITTLE FOOL?'

'I'm going over to Jimmy's uncle.'

His uncle, who was a Justice of the Peace and an experienced country gentleman of the colonial model, lived about fifteen minutes away. As soon as he heard the story he offered to drive over with his wife and arbitrate with Mr Grant. We drove back in two cars.

As soon as we got there Mrs Grant ran out with a hand of green bananas for the Justice's wife who had come with him. Whenever anyone had given me anything, a breadfruit or a hand of green bananas I would be thrilled, thanking them profusely but all this lady said was, 'Very nice. Put it in the car.'

My mother gave me a savage jab in the ribcage and hissed, 'PAY CLOSE ATTENTION TO THIS!'

Jimmy's uncle unhurriedly strolled around the entire yard discussing the views with Mr Grant in a pleasant tone of voice that betrayed no emotion.

'My Goodness, is that Malvern Park over there? Lovely man, and that's Ocho Rios isn't it?'

We all trailed behind like ladies in waiting and Mr Grant transformed into Uriah Heep – ever so humble he wrung his hands. This phase lasted about ten minutes. Then phase two began.

'Now Clement (that was Mr Grant's first name) I have two complaints against you. One, that you have had the lights connected illegally and that makes us liable for prosecution, you understand.'

'Yes Sah!'

'Two, Miss MacMillan tells me that you have brought too many people to live here. That young man, Devon, isn't it? He will stay and work for Miss MacMillan, at a salary, to be discussed and those two young boys will live here so that he has company, as he wouldn't want to be alone. Everyone else should be out of here by, shall we say, tomorrow. Do me a favour, leave the place exactly as you found it. There is one thing more. Miss MacMillan has brought out another lychee tree. Dig a large hole, I would say about three feet in diameter, place the plant carefully into it, without disturbing the root structure and every three days, do me a favour, give it some water.'

'Yes Justice. Yes Sah. Is that all Sah? Ah don't want yu to have anything in yu heart against me when yu leave here Sah.'

'Oh Clement, you know there could never be anything between us that couldn't be sorted out.'

I learned from that masterful demonstration of diplomacy what could have taken me six years to learn. Positively feudal, I thought but to ignore it was actually dangerous. Change of any kind was resented, resisted and totally unappreciated in St Ann.

I was the one who had to change:

You must never employ anyone from the village. The reason is you may have a dispute.

Too much friend not enough, one enemy, too much.

You must always be courteous and kind but from a distance. No involvement.

If anyone wants to borrow money, lend it immediately and write it off. Never mention it again.

I obeyed these rules and 'the artis lady' got the reputation for being 'mannersable'.

The two little boys that were designated to live at Rockfield were called Patrick (although his name was Dennis) and Bunny. They were nine years old and became a big part of my life.

Another person who was an important influence in my life was Burnett. He was my neighbour over at Geddes – a fantasy of a house about twenty minutes away. Burnett was a contemporary of my parents and had been the favourite dancing partner of the Governor's wife, Lady Molly Huggins, at my father's nightclub in the '40s. Being with him was like being in the black and white movies that I had seen so many of growing up. He looked just like George Sanders. He had been educated at Oxford, followed by a stint in the RAF. His conversation was an education for me. I met him at a wedding in the hills behind Kingston. As the guests walked up the road from the church to the reception at Blue Mountain Inn he fell into step with me and said, 'Rah-ther like the wine festival isn't it?'

I laughed and he invited me to his house in Kingston for dinner. I told my Mother that I had met this tall, elegant man who wore a cravat and a toupee (which shortly after that he abandoned to my joy).

'Burnett? I can't believe you are just meeting Burnett Webster.'

His house was beautiful – a period piece with exquisite proportions. We dined at a wonderful, round dining table inlaid with slices of richly coloured semi-precious stone, scalloping out from a huge blue circle of pure lapis lazuli in the centre. Dinner was a bowl of soup served with pepper sherry and dessert was a bowl of star apples. When the dessert came Burnett moaned, 'Oh Judy, I love star apples, I love how they look, I love how they feel, I love how they taste!'

That was exactly the same way I felt about them and as I ate my eyes also fed with utter pleasure on the harmonious room that so completely expressed the personality of its owner. I was green as grass in so many ways. The first time we went to dinner in a restaurant and he asked me what wine I liked I said that I like that one called 'Sichel'.

'Those are the shippers, dear.'

He invited me to go to Morocco with him. I asked my father what he thought and he said, 'Don't think about it anymore – just go, go, go, go, GO!'

We had a marvelous time and laughed right through the Draa Valley to la Gazelle d'Or. He told me the story of his life and we discovered that despite the difference in age we were soul mates and liked exactly the same things in life.

A skewer of roasted lamb in rosemary and a basket of dates bought at the side of the road was a great lunch to us. He was a gay man of his era. I mean by that that he was 'in the closet' but never made an embarrassing display of his preferences which restraint I appreciated very much. Whatever he was repressing, he did it privately.

When I returned, everyone that I mentioned the trip to said, 'What? *You* went to Morocco with Burnett Webster? That's the living money you know girl.'

I asked Burnett if it was true because I had replied to all of them, 'Don't be ridiculous, Burnett doesn't know where the next bowl of soup is coming from. He hasn't got a pot to piss in!'

I can hear his exhausted whooping laughter now, 'Well, dear, I'm not rich but I'm not exactly poor. Thank God!'

Burnett had a country house, which was visible on a hill about a half an hour's drive from Rockfield. When I had told him that I had bought the house he said, 'Wonderful! St

Ann will come back to life. You will paint pictures and I will serve tea!'

Now he stepped out of the car to see the place. Miss Cotter had been a recluse so no one in the area had been to Rockfield in twenty years. Patrick and Bunny, the little boys that Justice had decreed should live there, were sleeping on a mattress on the floor sharing a light cover and when he saw them he shouted, 'Put on a pot of water. These make excellent soup!'

They giggled and flashed their brilliant smiles liking him right away.

He walked slowly through the house expressing his opinions: 'Oh the enfilade, dear, the enfilade. I think you should simply have sitting room, after sitting room, after sitting room. Charming dear, charming. What I do detest about the place though dear, are all the boring views, from every single window. *Another* boring view!'

At the end of seven years together Jimmy said, 'Miss Mac it has taken me seven years to satisfy you.' At the end of ten years the first, fine, careless rapture was diminishing. We went on a trip to Europe that fanned back the flame and came home glowing after several weeks.

In Holland, the street cries were 'Hashish ... Marijuana ... Coca?' He would put one hand up and say, 'We are from Jamaica,' and they would slink away bowing deeply and murmuring, 'Oh, sorry, sorry to bother you.'

In Austria, we went to Bad Riechenhall to see an incredible nineteenth-century spa with a promenade and bandstand where people still 'took the waters' and breathed in their vapours. In Vienna, I spent the day in the Kuntshistoriche – one of the city's forty museums marveling again at the Bruegel's.

In Germany, Heidleburg, and Munich, he pointed out the scenes of many of his Casanova exploits – sliding down precipitous rooftops to escape irate husbands. In Italy, I absorbed the paintings at The Uffizi in Florence. We ended our trip in Greece. On the tiny island of Paros there were no hotels. The locals come down to the boat and take you home with them. We stayed with a family and when passing by, on the little whitewashed street to go home, their neighbours opposite invited us in. We spent the afternoon drinking enormous quantities of wine and food that it was impossible to refuse – dancing with them as they pulled in from the street more and more delighted tourists. Jimmy amused them, and me, with a perfect imitation of their dancing style (arched back with arms outstretched) and without a word of Greek we had the best time with those people. I wanted to give them a present to thank them.

'A bottle of wine?'

'No Miss Mac, they will think that their wine wasn't good enough.'

'What then?'

'We will give them a huge greeting card and have someone write in Greek how much we enjoyed meeting them.'

I loved Jimmy for his sensitivity especially with simple people because the greeting card in their language was the perfect thing to do.

We returned to Jamaica and I was at a peak of joy.

My father had been ill while I was away. The first day back was a Sunday. I spent the day with him and he laughed until he cried hearing about the trip and saying, 'Judy you have to write a book, this is too much.'

The next day he went back into hospital. One week later

he was dead. I plummeted through a trap door into a black hole with no bottom. I do not remember the first year of my life without my father. My bottomless grief was the beginning of the end of my relationship with Jimmy. My second childhood was over.

Unfortunately I had gotten a year older every year and so had Alexei but Jimmy had not. I was forty and having my first adult crisis. I doubted all my choices and paid a huge price for my carefree irresponsible decade.

When my relationship with Jimmy was over, in many ways it left me unfit for another relationship. My male Jamaican readers will immediately leap to the conclusion that it was the loss of 'Big Hood' that caused that but the women will understand. It's not the one that you drink the love potion with that you need for the long, hard, dusty road. I refer you to the myth of Amor and Psyche. Often we see the truth but we stay. I had stayed in a fool's paradise a long time but we linger there because it is so hard to leave.

I was in this shaky state when Hurricane Gilbert hit me right slam bam between the eyes.

9

Hurricane Gilbert

What nuh dead nuh tek it throw wey

Every Jamaican has a hurricane story. Hurricane Gilbert, in 1988, divided my life in two and I was never quite the same after that because in its wake, what had blown away along with the roof at Rockfield, were my illusions.

I can't remember how I heard that Gilbert was coming because I was at Rockfield without a radio or a telephone. Patrick, the young boy who had come to live there, may have been the one to bring the news. All I had time to do was have one piece of wood nailed across the most fragile eastern-facing room that was all windows. I shrugged my shoulders and drove off down the hill to go back to Kingston.

I had worked on the house six years on a shoestring that was more like a cobweb making every mistake in the book. Jimmy's excellent advice was to do only what absolutely had to be done.

'Miss Mac, yu could dash away six million dollars and it would still be de wrong way to do it. What difference does any of it make if you end up ruining the house?'

He was right. There were so many things that I would have changed if I had had the money that became my favourite things in the end. I am thinking here of a slightly askew window in my bedroom which I wouldn't want straight now for anything because it makes me smile.

The roof though was an essential that absolutely had to be done. I had patched the worst parts of it with shingles I'm sure were stolen. When Mr Hairs, my neighbour next door, at Winefield, saw them his hairline receded an inch and he said, 'But, my dear girl, these are terrible shingles – all sap. I doubt that you'll get more than seven years out of these.'

At the age of thirty, seven years sounded like a very long time to me.

'Oh that's great Mr Hairs, because in seven years I am going to be so rich I'll pave this roof in gold!'

She mad you know, smoke too much ganja. What a shame eh.

The truth is, I lay in bed many a night looking up at the ominous black cracks in the ceiling through which descended a continuous fall out of black dust. Talking on the hotline to God that I had inherited from my father, 'God? It's me, Judy Ann. You have to help me. I have no idea how to fix this roof. How will I ever afford it?'

On the day itself, I went to get my mother and we spent the hurricane holding the door to the verandah of my apartment in Kingston shut. We screamed together through the terrifying noise that a hurricane makes. Outside the glass door, I saw the top of a big tree disappear like magic and water shot through the shut windows between the redwood louvre blades. When the eye of the hurricane passed, all my neighbours in the building went outside and we chatted and giggled nervously in the eerie, utter calm for half-an-hour before racing back in for the finish. That's when the hurricane comes back from the other direction.

Rocky, my sweet Rottweiler sprang into the middle of my bed hoping for one dry spot.

My mother's house had lost most of its roof as had four other houses belonging to my family which were my responsibility to repair. All I could think about afterwards was Rockfield but the roads were impassable with blown down telephone poles and trees.

Three days after Gilbert, I went with Burnett who was going down to St Ann to see how his house had fared. He had a chauffeur to drive us and, with a container with gas, we set off. It is usually a two hour ride but it took us most of the day to get to his house because of the trees and debris in the road and the many detours we had to take.

Burnett's house wasn't too badly affected and as we walked around my nerves were frayed because I was now so close to Rockfield but still didn't know what had happened there.

'I'm sorry Burnett but if we don't go to Rockfield soon I may start howling and not be able to stop.'

'Get in the car, dear.'

The landscape on the way up the hill looked burnt – dark brown, colourless and as unfamiliar as the moon. When we drove in, at first glance the house looked all right and the huge thatch palm that Miss Cotter had worried about was still there. I kissed the ground, like my sister does when she sees Dadeland Mall in Miami, before I realised that half the roof was gone. Behind the house, the lovely detached building built as an annex, which was the only part of the place that had aesthetically pleasing proportions, had gone. The valley was littered with the lumber from that building, which I had planned to make my studio.

It was a bad blow but I was so grateful for what remained that the full enormity of what needed now to be done didn't quite hit me at first. It was some time later, maybe a week and only after arrangements had been put in place and materials ordered for my mother's roof and the other damaged houses that I drove out with my dog, Rocky, to repair mine. I had less than a thousand dollars in cash, a pack of candles, some matches and a container of water. Apart from Rocky I was alone. I cried the entire way.

Rain had poured into the house for a week. My hands shook as I started to clean up. I broke many things that had survived the hurricane with my shaking hands. The lost roof had damaged the water tank and the water had all drained away. As night came, I lit one of my few candles and went to the verandah where I often sat in the darkness to enjoy the night.

I sat on the verandah all night staring into the darkness. I don't know if it qualifies as prayer but it was certainly emanation. I felt a bottomless remorse. It was deeply painful, as painful as any grief I've ever experienced. I begged the Almighty God forgiveness for every act of cruelty I'd ever committed and my coldness, which had grown over the years, towards my mother. I felt that I had been punished and also that I deserved to be punished. Coming up to morning, I felt finally able to sleep and went into one room which had a roof and lay down.

I was awakened by the sound of rain and saw it seeping under the door of the room I was in. What happened after that was like being in an altered state. A calm as deep as the ocean filled my soul and like a friend it stayed with me all day. I drove out with my mind a blank and no plan beyond getting something to patch up that huge hole. My mind was wide open – completely open to the present. It was blank and washed clean. It felt blissful. It felt like rapture that I had never before experienced and have never experienced since.

At the bottom of the track I saw two men and asked them if they would come and fix my roof. They said they couldn't come now but they would come later. Everything seemed inevitable, even destined, in my state of absolute acceptance. The stillness was not outside. It was inside me.

I drove to the hardware store in the nearest little village. No, they didn't have any zinc. Unconcerned, I headed for Brown's Town which had a bigger hardware store. Along the way I had to pass Burnett's gate and saw Oscar, a man who worked for him, standing at the side of the road.

'Come with me, Oscar.'

Without a word he sat beside me in the car and we drove to Brown's Town in silence. What looked like thousands of people were all demanding zinc outside the hardware store. Oscar left me and I went round the back of the store into the backyard. I was standing there eating an orange for breakfast when a man materialised beside me. He said, 'What do you need?'

'Anything that will stop up a hole in my roof.'

He pointed to the used sheets of aluminum on the ground that I had been staring at and said, 'Will that do?'

Yes, but the price would have used up all the money I had. In that moment, Oscar appeared and seeing my hesitation pulled two blank cheques from his pocket signed by Burnett Webster. He said, 'Use them.'

They put the sheeting on a truck and I followed it back to Rockfield. I was beginning to glimpse the miraculous nature of the day and I was holding my breath because I never wanted the bliss that filled my soul to leave. The two men that I had seen earlier were standing on the lawn. I still had the cash so we arranged a price and they started work up there on the roof right away. The sheets of metal were the exact amount I needed without one foot left over.

I knew to the dollar how much money was in my handbag when two young girls from the village who I had been painting for about a year came up. I thought that since they had posed for me so many times for various paintings that they were concerned for me and I greeted them with joy.

'What happened at your house?'

'De roof come off but we put it back on.'

I asked one of them to turn the pages of one of my ruined art books in the sun while she was sitting on the step and went about gathering up things to give them to take home. I noticed without judgment that she didn't do it, she used the bathroom and very soon after they left. My handbag had been left in the bathroom and I discovered that the money was missing. Usually there would have been room for doubt, but not today. I drove down my hill and up the next to their house and when her mother came to the gate I said, 'Your daughters have robbed me and I cannot afford to be robbed today. Come with me and get back my money.'

She did not doubt me for a second; after all mothers know their children better than anyone else. All she said as she jumped into the seat beside me was, 'Children are a crosses, drive ah Mr Rowe, cowpen gate.'

That is exactly where the two girls were standing holding the bag of things I'd just given them.

Their eyes bulged when they saw their mother beside me in the car.

To them I said, 'Get in the car and give your mother that bag.'

To their mother I said, 'Find my money.'

She handed it to me and I told those girls that I never ever wanted to see their faces again. I subsequently gave away every drawing I had done of them to various hurricane relief fund raising efforts.

By evening the hole in the roof was almost completely covered. If you know Jamaica even a little bit, you will know that the impossible had been achieved. Much more than that had happened though in my life that day. I had seen the reality of my life with complete clarity. I had not really known before that I was alone and that anything else is an illusion. But in that understanding had come a miraculous experience of Grace and I never felt fear at being alone again. I had been in my shattered house shoveling debris for about a week when the English insurance assessor drove up my hill. He found the classic mad woman. I had matted hair, dirty feet and bloody hands because I had been cutting up liver for the dog. Only an Englishman could have kept his face composed with the sight that I was that day. He walked around and assessed that the company were liable only to give me twelve thousand Jamaican dollars. I had increased the insurance on all the other properties I had to look after belonging to my family but had forgotten my own house.

He threw me a lifeline and said, 'If you reinsure with us to the full value of the house, I'll cover you anyway.'

That is how I got a new roof for the house.

'One hundred shingles to a bundle. Four bundles to a square. A square is ten by ten.'

Many years later when I needed a roof again I would say to friends, please don't mention it to God though because last time I asked him for help and he slightly overdid it.

I was changed in another crucial way. The good always comes with bad. I was over forty years old before I realized that the village people, whom I had found so lovable did not necessarily return my emotions. If they could rob me on a day like that with everything shattered around me then they didn't see me as a human being just like them.

Bitterness entered my heart and painting has no worse enemy than bitterness. It shows up just like a stain. I stopped painting portraits. Heartbroken, I didn't think that I would ever be able to paint portraits as I had before when my illusions were intact. I turned to still life and flower studies after Gilbert.

I had faced the reality of my life but knowing it was not necessarily a good thing for me. I entered a period I call 'my tunnel'. I withdrew from life. It happened so gradually that I did not even notice what was happening until the sides of the tunnel were overgrown and bushy and had narrowed so much that there seemed no way out.

After Gilbert, eleven village people, employees of the man who owned the surrounding land came to live in the two outbuildings at the back and they made any desire to hold on to illusions quite impossible. The land that came with Rockfield was only an acre and a third. It did not include these outbuildings that were so close. Up until that time two cattle-penners had lived in one each and we had maintained perfectly harmonious relations.

It was interesting that when women came there, the men started to abuse me but if I passed them on the road, without witnesses, they would sometimes give an involuntary wave – a friendly reflex action from the past. It was clear to me that the abuse was to impress their women, to demonstrate that I was not to be treated any better than they were. One day I was standing near to the little barbed wire fence that separated the two yards. One of the women, a round-faced pretty girl, said indicating my side of the fence.

'Ah see a man widout a ead ovah dere.'

I turned around in a mock performance of looking, and turned back to her, 'You saw a man without a head standing in this garden?'

She nodded her head slowly like a sage and smiled a flashing wicked smile. Her ackee-seed eyes were huge in that childish face.

'Well, the difference between us is that, if I saw a man without a head I would have to be put in hospital for the rest of my life but you seem to be fine.'

I smiled pleasantly but falsely and went inside dismissing this childishness, which was in the same category as a mosquito bite. But have you ever been bitten by lots of mosquitoes?

I would awake at dawn to the sound of their quarrels.

'Bumbo-claat! Ras claat! Pussy-claat! Blood-hole! Blood-seed! Pussy-hole! Dis claat and dat, claat, claat, claat!'

I would sigh and marvel to myself that the exquisite surroundings could be the setting for so much rage. Even the pumpkins on a vine in my backyard, lying close to the fence were stabbed with a machete so that they would spoil. Everything left outside the house itself that could be lifted disappeared. One morning – a sacred time to me – while drinking a cup of coffee, I saw a man urinating from the outside staircase of the little building down to the ground. Worse still, I was observed and commented on with that 'chanting-on-the-wind' in words that I was not meant to understand.

'She ovah dere wid anadda white man again.'

One day there was an escalation. One of the men, let's call him Mean, advanced towards me shouting and with his arm raised, 'Yu RED an yu MAWGER!'

'Both music to my ears.'

I am not my mother's daughter for nothing. I advanced towards him forcing him to step back towards the boundary saying in a perfectly calm voice.

'Mean, you are on my land. I have a legal right to live without abuse on this piece of land that I have paid for. You get off my land *right now*.'

When he reached the perimeter though he was still too close for comfort. Clearly, I needed a bigger piece of land and that would come. This morning though I jumped in the car and drove down to the police station in St Ann's Bay.

As I stepped into the station a policeman was lovingly polishing an enormous rifle. I slipped seamlessly into my little old, colonial lady, *who can't mash ants*, performance.

'Oh my, *what* a lovely big gun. Oh boy, I wish I had a gun like that! You think you could come up to my place and help me with some people who are giving me a warm time up there?'

'Ah don't 'ave no vee-hickle.'

'Well, I do.'

'I am not allowed to go in your vehicle.'

I was shown into the Superintendent's office.

He was a dear, portly old gentleman who, after hearing my story, said that he would come and speak to Mean and the gang at the back.

When he had finished speaking to them he came over to me.

'Miss MacMillan, I have admonished and discharged.'

As we sat having coffee, I thanked him for his assistance and unburdened myself a bit about how distressing I found it all – the urinating especially – and he said, 'Miss MacMillan, you may need to sit in another chair when you have coffee.'

With a shock, I saw that he was right but the fact that this had not occurred to me showed that I was definitely becoming unhinged.

Then there were the gardeners. I had a series of gardeners working for me. I could live without a man to take me to dinner, to make love to me and to protect me. But one man you cannot live without in rural Jamaica is a gardener.

One of these, with every utterance, revealed a mind in which negativity spiraled-down so alarmingly, that I shuddered to follow his thinking. I fancied that I might arrive at a crossroad and have a face to face encounter with Legba himself. Let's call him Grandolph the Informer.

One day as I was watching from my kitchen window, a child of the gang at the back jumped over the fence and hopped like a rabbit through the back garden to pinch a pepper from the tree in my backyard. I asked Grandolph, 'Why don't they just throw a pepper in the ground, they wouldn't even have to water it, in no time at all it would grow and they would have their own pepper tree?'

'Becaw they might 'ave to leave 'ere, and somebaddy else would get the pepper dem.'

So what I wondered if some one else got something you had no use for?

Grandolph refused to water newly planted trees.

'Dat hard fe dead, Miss Judy, hard fe dead.'

Or weed.

'The weed dem keep de 'ert cool.'

I had tried to exorcise my own negative feelings about Grandolph by doing a series of portraits of him. A long time after he worked for me he returned one day to say that he had planted a plantain tree while there and had come for some plantains. My new friend, Inell, was on her first visit to Rockfield. She threw a cold glance at him in the doorway and – looking like the Queen of Sheba – pronounced the first of many judgments that I was to be increasingly grateful for.

'Judy, tell him to take his tree and go.'

I had heard about Inell from a mutual friend. Apparently,

while still very young and on a schoolteachers pay, she had built her own house in secret. I asked to meet her because I was intrigued, so I was included at an afternoon tea party – just like the ones my mother used to have. Inell was so beautiful that I immediately wanted to paint her and also asked the question, 'Why did you build your house in secret?'

'Because most people are so negative that if they had known about it they would have stopped me.'

This was a person who had learned to function against the magnetic pull of forces that have formed themselves into a status quo in Jamaica. A word about these forces.

Everyone on the island knows about and lives in spite of these forces, which we call by the generic term 'Bad Mind'. I call it 'cockroach mentality'. The 'Bad Mind Brigade' combine and attack wherever their sensors detect laughter, joy or success. A project that has any hope of a successful outcome must be kept hidden from them. If a swarm of cockroaches pick up a positive energy, they will join forces to correct the situation. Anything that one cockroach gets is seen as unfairly snatched from the jaws of other cockroaches. A folksong expresses the phenomenon perfectly:

'Mi want 500 feet of board
Far to build up mi firewall higher
Far my neighbour have some long mout pickney
Jus a peeping on mi pot pon fire.

Lawd a massy mercy Lawd
Is enough to mek man hollar
Far mi neighbour have some dry foot pickney
Jus a peeping on mi pot pon fire.'

But the 500 feet of board is never enough to safeguard privacy from this continuous inescapable scrutiny. The desire for escape can reach to levels of paranoia.

Nuh mek you right han know what you left han is doing.

I started some drawings of Inell and we found that we had a great deal in common.

My friends invariably turn out to be Daddy's girls who, no matter how feminine they appear on the surface, are un-cowed women who think for themselves and have no doubts about deserving the best from life. Refreshingly, she was not embarrassed about her rural upbringing and when she spoke about her childhood – the memories of roasting cashews on a sheet of hot zinc or grinding fresh roasted coffee beans – were as evocative as poetry. She had a horrendous hurricane Gilbert experience and, like me, had faced her 'aloneness' then too. She became a loyal confidant with a mind that leaned towards what my mother called 'executive skills' in the exact ratio to my lack of them. She had never smoked a cigarette let alone herbs so her memory was astonishing. It was like having a friend who was partly a computer. I told her everything in order to store it.

I would say, 'Inell, did I enter the National Gallery show last year? Because I am reading a review here and forty-five artists are mentioned but there is no mention of my painting.'

'Don't you remember? You entered the big landscape of pastures from the back of Rockfield?'

She never let me slip back into unquestioned, inherited attitudes.

'Isn't it shocking that these people have no running water in their houses?'

'Who are you calling 'these people' Judy? Don't patronise

them. They love running down to the standpipe. It's where they meet their friends.'

Inell opened up a huge new picture window into modern Jamaica.

But my trouble with gardeners continued. Firing a gardener was an enterprise so dangerous that it didn't bear thinking about. You had to mine deep down to a subterranean level, requiring huge reserves of trickery, guile and deceit worthy of Anansi. The trick was to get him to leave without firing him. I had no desire to get my head chopped off with the machete that I had seen sever the guava tree with one stroke.

I had a drunk called, Myron, working for me after Grandolph the Informer. He was wonderful when sober and loved to grow things. As soon as I opened my kitchen windows on arrival he would place something delicious that he had grown on the windowsill. We got along really well but as nice as he was when sober when he was drunk it was scary.

One dark rainy day, I was in my tiny studio where I had been painting some wild lemons. Suddenly I heard a loud stomping sound, heavy footsteps coming through the house. Alarmed, I looked up to see Myron positively heaving in the doorway of the small room. He looked like a dragon with a frightening, enraged look on his face. I said as sharply as I could, 'Go to your room!

Gwey! Yu ole drunkard yu

He shot off like a mongoose and all my courage left me. I locked up the house and went upstairs to my bedroom wailing inside. Outside the rain and wind made the house tremble as I pulled the covers up over my head calling out on my hotline.

'God, you see my life on top of this hill. You see me here, with the damn place wuthering around me and a wild man drunk out of his mind as my only protection.'

I railed against fate and fell asleep exhausted. In the morning I packed my bag and slipped out to escape to Kingston, which paradoxically – crime capital as it was supposed to be – was my haven from rural Jamaica. On my return, I met a former neighbour from the days when I had lived in my townhouse in Kingston. At the time she had been married to a sixties-style black radical, who had not allowed her to come to my house where I was always inviting her to play backgammon. Dressed in African clothes, she would breastfeed her production line babies on the lawn of the common area. Once, when she was expecting twins I offered her a crib that Alexei had outgrown but was still in perfect condition and she said, 'Do you know how many children in the ghetto sleep five in a crib?'

'Yes but not by choice. I think if someone gave them a crib they would take it.'

I'm pretty sure that her husband would not allow her to accept my crib if he would not allow her to play backgammon.

I was glad to see her again now free from her oppressor husband. Terrified that I was turning into a racist, I confessed to her my dislike of the rural people who had become snakes in my paradise. I'll never forget her honesty.

'You know Judy, that in those days when we first met, poor black people were sacred to me. Richard and I bought a place in the country and tried to live there and grow our own food. Every time I looked out the window I saw someone leaving with a bag of my crop. It didn't matter how black I was, to them I was a white woman living in a big house. At the end of a year I applied for a gun license.

I gasped. Would she have shot at them?

'Gladly.'

I'm not a Roman Catholic but after this straight talking I

felt as if I'd gone to confession and received expiation. I started painting portraits again including one of the best I have ever done. It took four years to complete. It was without illusions and it was all the better for that. I called it, *Mas Joe on Sunday*. So there were cracks of light in my tunnel too. It wasn't all darkness.

My gardener problem was solved after hiring someone that worked for a friend, Bill Schickler, who lived close by. Bill was a retired American and he provided the umbrella of male authority for me. I paid him and he paid my gardener. So the gardener was really not working for me – a woman – which was way below his dignity. For years after Bill died, that umbrella continued to protect me just as the rural etiquette that I had learned from Jimmy never let me down. It kept me safe all those years I painted in the wilderness, long after our relationship was over.

In the end though I bought the piece of land at the back. The day that my hired truck, piled high with all the garbage, drove off down the hill leaving the land just as it had been before, I felt weak with joy. To celebrate, I painted a Poinciana tree that had been tormented with bits of old zinc nailed around her trunk. Nowadays, the birds that I love most nest there – a big family of sparrow hawks. And at the time of writing, dear Mr Chisholm, my gardener and my caretaker, happily lives and works at Rockfield.

10

Kenny and Chris

Good friend better than pocket money

During the years of doubt after my father's death there was a strong pull from the past, a desire to go back to a safer, more conventional time. Occasionally, I reached out to the people I had lost touch with – the protected women with husbands and families and the traditional Jamaican lifestyle that I was supposed to have had. Yet the path back was blocked as the nature of my intense relationship with art and my occupation as an artist had compounded my misfit status. I had fallen through the social cracks. There was a blanket explanation. That question, 'Are you still doing the painting?' separated me. Maybe they felt that I had rejected the singers but I had only rejected the song.

A word here about these wives. I was always a little amused that they guarded their husbands as assiduously as a Rottweiler imagining that all women were after them.

Every John Crow tink him pickney white

I spanked a number of straying husbands on their bottoms and sent them home to their wives but you can never anticipate in Jamaica. Everything is inverted in this land where plastic leaks and fast food is slow. So there was something worse than wanting another woman's husband and that was not wanting him. The wives, many of whom had never driven to Ocho Rios by themselves, could be forgiven for finding my life strange as

I had started combining figures and landscape – sometimes taking my models out on location with me. It looked, even to other painters, as if I were deliberately making life hard for myself. Colin would say disdainfully, 'Judy doesn't think she's painting unless she is hanging off a cliff somewhere.'

But I wanted the viewer to feel as if they were actually there having the experience with me and the only way to achieve that was by living it. Looking at visual information in a small glossy photograph just didn't do it for me.

Painting from nature is not relaxing. It's tense. The mind is speeding on a abstract tightrope of line, tone, colour, drawing, shape, texture and scale, while the hand clumsily, frustratingly tries to keep up.

A stream of subliminal commands comes from within: change the oil; wipe the brush; switch to the sable; use the knife; add more white. As automatic as a pulse, these become techniques that are individual to each painter, evolving from a personal need, a need that is almost religious in nature. As my practice deepened I learned my own way – keeping this, discarding that and making little discoveries. For example, glazing too much deadened the surface while little accidental marks gave it life – even the bits of dry grass that attached to the canvas in the bush or sand from the beach. The concentration has to be built up over years. At first I could only concentrate for two hours in a session, then three and finally five. But on rare occasions I went for seven hours and those were great days.

Mastery was when you could enter the zone of concentration at will and maintain it. I needed to be fit. Any stale tiredness hung over from the night before worked against it and so, like an athlete, I made sure I was always fresh for the next day's work.

Artis, teach me de wuk!

It can make you crazy. I developed an eccentric habit of sneaking up on my paintings – trying to catch them unaware when I brought them inside. It was then that I 'saw' them for the first time. Until that moment I only saw what was in front of my eyes in that light outside. Another trick was placing the canvas at the foot of my bed so, in that first moment of sight in a new day, I could ambush the flaws hidden in the camouflage to which my eyes had become so accustomed. Looking at the picture reversed in a mirror had the same effect.

Painting is difficult, maddeningly so. You face your inadequacies every day but it's magical too. I would turn it around and suddenly look and hear my own involuntary intake of breath as what I had been looking at for so long suddenly leapt from my canvas. When that happened – and it didn't happen always – it was a feeling like nothing else on earth. It was experiencing life on a more intense level and it made it worthwhile.

Once on a public beach, I had set the model up in the water and was just about sitting in the water myself to paint. The bane of my existence were my spindly little portable easels which were completely unable to cope with sand and wind blowing. They necessitated borrowing a heavy weight from a dreadlocked fisherman who was watching all these antics from a row of shacks. When I finished, now covered in paint and with my hair like Medusa, I returned his coal stove. He explained me to his neighbours, 'Artis yu know, shi wild, she wild, shi wild, shi wild. Shi wild.'

A great many of my old friends had left in the exodus. When I walked into a living room in London and expatriate Jamaicans were present, there were loud horrified cries.

'Are you still *down there*? Are you crazy? Are you waiting to be murdered in your bed?'

I told them a story: a man from the street had stuck his

head into the window of my car in downtown Kingston and with a face distorted with hatred, snarled, 'White *pussy*!'

I looked right into his eyes and answered mildly, 'Why yu suh miserable today? Who trouble yu?'

He started to smile sheepishly, looked embarrassed and said in a rather pathetic way, 'Heh heh heh, Ah like white pussy.'

'Yes, well, fine.'

So my audience found me strange too and would not accept how simply the hostility they feared could be disarmed. Where would I begin to explain to them that in those early ecstatic years I slept with my bedroom windows open to the night breeze. Or that in my heart I was singing the plaintive words, 'I man born ya, I nah leave ya, pot ah boil ya, belly full ya.'

Shi mad yu nuh. Smoke too much ganja.

In expat Miami, conversation focused on the latest shocking stories from Jamaica and usually slipped into the nostalgia of the days before Manley.

Cho, I remember a goal I made for Manning's Cup yu si man.

They devoured the overseas edition of the local newspaper raking through for evidence that supported their decision to leave and using these as a club for my obstinate head. They ate more canned ackee than they had ever eaten before when they had the real thing. I avoided them as much as possible. I didn't want to apologise for the fact that I still loved Jamaica anymore than I wanted to be shamed for painting its beauty. I reached out at this time to new friends and they were almost all foreigners and gay people. I would have been very lonely had it not been for my gay friends.

In fact, the best marriage I ever saw was between two men.

I met Kenny and Chris through a mutual Jamaican friend – the photographer, Cookie Kinkead – at a weekend house party in

Bridgehampton, New York. By the time we all got on the train back to Manhattan, we were friends but I never imagined at the time what an important relationship had begun. After that casual meeting they offered me the use of their empty apartment in Greenwich Village in the way that Jamaicans, with our strong tradition of hospitality, do as a matter of course many times a year. I was very used to invitations of reciprocity but, for me, it was the first time that Americans had offered me hospitality first. They were separately visiting their families, prior to leaving New York, in order to live together in San Francisco. Everyday they called to ask what we were doing and to give insider advice.

'Judy, don't let her take you to the Cubby Hole no matter what she says.'

Soon after my return to Jamaica, Cookie called from America and asked me to look after them in Jamaica on their vacation. She wasn't able to leave New York and feared her house in Jamaica, which had been locked up for months, would be full of an alarming number of dead insects. Happy to reciprocate, I collected them at the Montego Bay airport and drove them to Rockfield. Kenny's screams, when we drove in, were frightening but they were screams of delight not horror. He had never left the United States before and his amazed response to the simple things we took for granted were great fun – like buying a coconut and having the seller chop open a fresh one from the very tree that he was sitting under. This was the 1980s, when all that the rural supermarkets offered were bottles of syrup, cornmeal, rice and – if one was really lucky – suspicious looking cuts of meat and rolls of strangely coloured, coarse toilet paper.

Tun yu han mek fashion

Kenny spun around the rusty Claremont supermarket in

shocked silence without breaking his stride. But they loved staying at Rockfield so much that after awhile, and uniquely among my houseguests, they 'knew the runnings' so well that I could leave them on that hill without a worry. I knew they would be having their showers for fun in the waterfall of a nearby river or working in the garden and happily pottering with that almost organic 'fix-it' talent that Americans often have at their fingertips. I would return from Kingston to find an organised house with hooks set up for small tools on the wall of the kitchen with a sign made by Chris, who was learning the language.

'HERE DEM PUT.'

'Judy, I changed this lock for you but I wished halfway that I hadn't started. When I took the old one off, the wood under it looked like a piece of Swiss cheese.'

Chris operated in Jamaica as if he was born there. I had no telephone at the house.

'Judy, if you ever get a phone in this house I will never speak to you again.'

So he was completely out of touch with his real estate office in San Francisco yet found it truly relaxing. Once, after several days of being incommunicado, he called his office from a little phone booth at the edge of a gully while Kenny and I waited for him in the Jeep. I would have hesitated calling Kingston even if I had the handfuls of coins required but after awhile he joined us with, 'closed the deal.'

The only offers to consider in Jamaica were whether to have his hair plaited or to have an aloe vera massage – two of the few services available in the area at the time. In response to these offers he would say, 'Awww you just want me to look like a stupid white man.'

He loved shopping in the market in St Ann's Bay where as

soon as he appeared the cry would go up, 'Ah de Don, Ah de Don! Ah de money dat! Step ovah here Don. What yu looking today?'

From his purchases, he would concoct delicious versions of the local dishes. This turned every meal into an entertainment and they were visually appealing enough to photograph before eating. We gathered wild plants from our hikes through the countryside and they filled the house with extraordinary arrangements of wild orchids and bromeliads – flowers that we considered too humble for use inside.

Ah de wild pine dat she have inna de dining hall?

And so they became Jamaica addicts, making several visits a year and contributed greatly to the development of Rockfield – always leaving it better than they found it and setting 'homework' for me before leaving.

'I want you to get four Royal Palms put them there, there, there and there. Got that? O.K. and I want four Christmas palms over there and put in a tropical garden all the way down this slope.'

Lawd Miss Judy, what a way the place would look nice if dey would stay a munt!

I knew nothing about gardening. Even if the lawn covered the roof in those days, I would leap out of the car, sweep out the house and start painting.

On their first visit, after a few days Chris asked in the measured tones they always used with me, as if they were speaking to someone who had had a lobotomy, 'Judy Ann, do you have a *garden clipper?*'

I handed him a brand new pair still in its case and saw that significant look they so often exchanged – a shared wavelength that did not need words. My instructions began: 'Now Judy

Ann, I want you to clip off all the dry pieces of this plant right down as far as you can, and every week give it a little *wadder*.'

When they left, I continued for days and obediently clipped my formal garden right down to the ground. Although covered in scratches and cuts, I couldn't stop because under all the weeds I found, with growing excitement, beds full of daylilies, sago palms, dahlias and nasturtiums that had been there all the time – like a badly wrapped present.

They were the kind of guests one is always sorry to see leave and we all know how rare those are.

'Judy Ann, why is that man outside the bar over there smiling at me and holding on to his cock?'

'He doesn't know he is holding on to his cock. He just does that all day. He is smiling because he is friendly. He has no idea that you are gay.'

Hear dat? Batty man yu know

For my part, I liked that they seemed to have no concept of doing without things. It was a refreshing escape from the prevailing poverty mentality.

'There are no grapefruit for the vodka and grapefruit cocktails.'

'Well, do without grapefruit. We have oranges.'

'Do without *grapefruit*? Why? I'm in Jamaica!'

On a call, when they were back in San Francisco, I would hear, 'Judy, I left the house for work this morning and when I came back there was a garden with grass, full-grown trees and flowers where only dirt had been before. Kenny ordered it and they put it all in in one day.'

This sort of instant gratification was an invigorating contrast to Jamaica where everything took so long. This is mainly because all the energy that should go into a job was usually diverted into destabilizing the job in order to get out of doing the job. No amount of money could help you out of that spiral.

I started going to visit them in California every year, usually in the spring to paint the flowers. The America that I experienced with them was a total rewrite of my first experience of Ohio.

Suh, how she get dat now?

I would arrive broken – worn out by the difficulties of my life in Jamaica – and rehabilitation would begin immediately: I never drove a car; I never made a decision; I didn't have to think; I didn't have to function. I was a child again. Typically they would collect me at the airport and place me in the back of the car. I would hear them discussing me, this cowed, punished creature, 'Let's see if we can do something with her hair.'

'I'll make an appointment tomorrow.'

Later at the hairdressers, 'Did you see her hair when she came in here? If you were on the *street* you saw it!'

On my first visit, when I saw the panoramic view of the city from the wide-glassed front of their apartment I sighed, 'How I would love to paint this.'

'Well why don't you?'

'Because I couldn't do it in a week.'

'So stay as long as it takes to do it.'

It was a great experience doing that painting. It was a complicated composition because the tall skyscrapers of the city were in the distance, with sky and sea behind them. In front of that backdrop were two natural untouched hills with trees and grass and at their base were the small higgledy-piggledy Victorian buildings and streets that spread forward until one was looking down at their rooftops. As the big things were in the distance and the small things in the foreground, the scale was difficult to make convincing and the city intermittently disappeared behind mist and loomed out of it again in a surreal way.

It took a month to do and I was allowed to work exactly as if I was at home: they did not break my trance; they did not force me to talk; they did not mind if I called them by the wrong names.

It's always fascinating for me to get the perspective right. It requires a lot of measurement, drawing and re-drawing but I do not find it tedious because the accuracy gives the image so much power. Passing through the streets that I had seen from my viewpoint above, I would recognise the blue building with the onion dome or the pale yellow one with white fretwork and so got to know that part of city just by painting it.

It was my habit to work on several paintings at the same time so, as a change from the big one, I also did two small portraits of Kenny and Chris. When I was putting in finishing touches to the cityscape, Chris asked if I could make one of the skyscrapers the same height as the tallest building in the group. It was a matter of two tiny strokes of paint.

'No problem, but why?'

'Because I think that my client would like that!'

He sold the painting to a client – whose office was in the adjusted building – for her boardroom. It was a liberating thing to have happened because there was no Jamaican connection and from this beginning a small American clientele started to develop.

One one cocoa fill basket

On that first trip, an experienced waitress would take one look at my rapt face and to my relief not address me at all because they could talk faster than I could think.

'What does the girl want?'

Once a man joined us from another table and when Chris

ordered for me he said, 'An American woman would never allow that.'

'Yes, but Judy Ann *likes* to be taken care of.'

He would ask me, 'Do you like oysters?'

'No. They are among the very few things that I've put in my mouth that I don't like.'

When a huge platter of oysters were put on the table for the others, the waitress whispered to me, 'Your caviar will be here in a minute.'

I thought that American women were missing out.

Kenny took charge of my appearance. On one occasion, as soon as we entered the house from the airport, he pulled a chair up: his knees were touching my knees; his hands holding mine tightly; his eyes staring deeply into mine as if he was planning to hypnotise me and said, 'Judy Ann, you must promise me that you will never, ever, ever wear a pair of black Reeboks again unless you are going into the *fields*. In this country sneakers are white. Only *big bull dykes* wear black Reeboks.'

And so he would direct me to some backless, black and white high-heeled pumps such as Marilyn Monroe would have worn.

'I can't walk in those. I used to once but I've lost the ability to walk in them.'

'You will walk in them and you will like it even if your feet are bleeding stumps.'

He often repeated my remark that I'd learned more about how to be a woman from him than I had ever learned from a woman. It was tongue in cheek but his pleasure revealed that to these men to be feminine was a compliment, not an insult. In fact the very best thing about being in America was their respect for women.

Between my first American experience and my second, attitudes to women in Jamaica had gone through enormous changes. It was partly because the style of the tenement yards had been enshrined as 'culture'. Also it was a backlash of resentment for the new equality of women internationally. But whatever the reason one had to live with the results.

The American women who had fought beside their men in those covered wagons had earned, for all their sisters that came afterwards, a respect that for me was as sweet as a drink of cold water when I came in from painting in the heat. The enormous contribution of American women to their society was ongoing and often took bizarre forms. Certainly, it was at odds with the feminism of my green youth or my readings of Germaine Greer and Simone de Beauvoir. I had weighed the truth of their words against my mother's tears but they looked like a pale watercolour in comparison to this vibrant parade of thickset lesbians at their annual 'Gay Parade'. They marched with greasy hair and nasty black T-shirts, chanting in unison, 'We are the DYKES FROM HELL. We've crossed the line and we'll do it again!'

My own feminist experience had been sabotaged during what we can call the 'Jimmy days'. Yet, ironically, in those days I *was* considered a feminist. One day sitting at a table in a cafe beside Mr Machismo, a trendy young miss came up to me and, ignoring Jimmy, as if he were thin air said, 'Judy Ann, we are having a march for women's rights. We want you to join us.'

Before I could answer Jimmy said, 'Why yu marching sweet heart, can't get a good man to love yu?'

'Oh God, seriously Judy Ann, we are marching between Cross Roads and Half-Way Tree and it starts at four o'clock in the morning.'

'Four o'clock in the morning? Miss Mac can't go. At four

o'clock in the morning Miss Mac has to lie down and take cock.'

I wanted the ground to open up and swallow me. To make matters worse, his remark became legendary. Even at the drive-in cinema my friends would spot me from a far-away car and yell, 'Miss Mac what are you doing here? Go home, lie down and take cock!'

However, on the US mainland, it was explained to me that mass theatre in the form of these events was necessary to force change. And certainly all the major politicians, including the mayor, took part in the Gay Parade as the size of the vote made it impossible to ignore. I was impressed: it was 'freedom' but a structured freedom. They had their day and they had their say – all with the protection of the police and the tolerance of the city behind them. The quiet domestic life of my friends: with its celebration of the seasons; the unwrapping of Christmas ornaments and hot dogs on the Fourth of July was as far from these bizarre displays as it was possible to be. Witnessing their every day lives, along with the other gay people who became dear to me, was enjoyable enough to put their sexual choices way down on the list of things of importance.

To me the arrangements of American lives were like a fragile house of cards. The removal of one card – a change of time for someone to come to work – could so totally unbalance the whole that the information would be communicated instantly so that another card could be put in its place. The house of cards was held up by a shared consensus of commitments and appointments, all structured around time. Things were taken literally. Saying what one meant and doing what one said was such a soothing respite from the perplexing kaleidoscope of ever shifting systems that is Jamaica. On the island there is no concept for wasting time because time is seen as unlimited.

Over and over I would say, 'How did you know to go there?'

'Because the sign said so.'

Where I came from I never read signs because they had no meaning. One sign in Jamaica was beside the window for getting a visitor's visa to England at the Office of The British High Commission. It read, 'If you are visiting Britain this summer you do not need an entry permit.'

And directly below, 'If you enter Britain this summer without an entry permit you may be sent home,'

Meanwhile, at the tax office you went to the 'Land Valuation' window to license your car. And at the post office window, a sign that said 'STAMPS', did not mean that you could buy a stamp there. As a consequence I hadn't read a sign in years.

Just as I had shared the inside Jamaica experience, they shared the working America that you must know to understand that country.

I was there a lot during the first year in the city when there was almost no business for Chris – the new boy on the block. I saw his demonstration of stoicism and sheer, cool grit that I have never forgotten. I never respected anyone more than Chris.

Everyday he would leave for work dressed in an immaculate Armani suit, to a building so elegant it was cited as an example of cutting edge architectural design. The office itself, decorated by Kenny in perfect taste, had to be a living example of what the company could do for the client. It was serene and perfectly ordered: from the fresh flowers in the foyer every day; to the gleaming paneling of the lifts and the Juan Miro lithograph on the wall. Every evening he would return.

'Any business?'

'Nope.'

The result of my labour was always tangible. You could hang it on a wall.

'What do you really do in there?'

'I try to get people who already have leases to break their lease and come to us.'

'How do you do it?'

'Well, I had a little gold ingot made with the words 'Credit Suisse' engraved on it and sent it to the owner of the best office building in the city with a note that said, 'Wouldn't you like to have them in your building?'

'Nice.'

'Yes, he called me within an hour.'

Meanwhile, Kenny had a pet store in Pacific Heights. His Easter hat parade for dogs made the news every year with its parade of exotic pets: a black bowler hat perhaps on a Rottweiler or a manicured poodle so fetching in chiffon. The merchandise was a big part of the fun of popping in. There were oriental rugs on the floor, crystal bowls, Burberry raincoats and flavouring for dry cereal packaged like vintage wines. You could buy a dog bed in any style to suit the décor of your house: deco; rococo; African kente cloth or traditional English chintzes. He would show them with a flourish saying, 'And the whole thing goes in the washer and dryer.'

There were sanitary napkins for dogs and hand-tooled leather collars from France. A parade of amazing breeds passed through on leashes with their owners. Complimentary dog biscuits in bowls were placed on the oriental rugs and chic girls arrived on time for their nail clipping appointments.

I would lie unseen in the back room recovering from home where the average dog gets a stone thrown at it for no reason at all and listen to their conversation.

'Ken, can you help? We have a Labrador who has been a

part of our family for eight years. Recently we got a new puppy and the Labrador has started shitting in the house.'

'I can fix that for you in one visit. Your dog just needs to feel wanted again. My fee is sixty dollars an hour.'

Kenny said to me when I was painting a portrait of him, 'Judy, I know the type of dog that would be perfect for your life. He would come with you in the bush. He would patrol the perimeter on your place in the country. You would never have to close a window or door at Rockfield again. Go home and order a Rottweiler and when he is six months old I'll come down and train him for you.'

Nervously, I did as he said. I was certain that I would take good care of the animal but afraid that I wouldn't really love it. When I picked up my puppy though, I felt that surge of joy, which is always confirmation to me that I am doing the right thing.

It was exactly as he described: for ten years, until he died, Rocky and I were inseparable and he remains one of my great loves.

Whenever I arrived in San Francisco they would take me to dinner at fashionable little bistros, with urban people whose problems all seemed to be about finding a parking space in the city. To them, my survival stories sounded like Chekhovian fables from a past world and it would send them into waves of hysterical laughter.

At the end of the nineties, Kenny and Chris bought a second house for weekends in the Napa Valley. It was a log house and charming because it was not decorated with moose heads on the walls but more like an English country cottage. There was a vineyard on one side and a little river on the opposite border. There were also two cottages on the property.

One of these became a studio for me when they commissioned a painting for the new house. It was right after returning from one of my regular painting pilgrimages (this time to Holland for a Vermeer show) and I thought it would be nice to do a big vanitas for the dining room. I was inspired by the Seventeenth Century Dutch still lifes, which are meant to express all the pleasures of worldly things – all the good things of life.

So it had roses from Kenny's spectacular garden and a cornucopia of fruits and vegetables. A little herb stalk was included in the painting because one of Kenny's worldly pleasures was his 'likkle' draw at a quarter to five each day, which is the international smoker's hour – rather like a cocktail at six for drinkers.

An elaborate composition, the painting took about a month to complete with weekends off when they joined me from the city bringing with them a menagerie of animals. As soon as it was completed they commissioned another, a landscape of the river for Chris's birthday. During the course of the two paintings they came up with a plan for me to be their artist in residence and stay six months working for an exhibition. I would simply work as I did at home and make no attempt to sell paintings in the area.

I had tried by this time to live at Rockfield full time, which had been my deferred dream until Alexei no longer needed Kingston for his schooling. I could have simplified my life and cut my expenses by having only one house to maintain. The experiment lasted seven months but ended with me hurriedly scratching one dream off the list. Strong as I was, stronger than I had ever intended or wanted to be, I wasn't strong enough to live permanently in the isolation of Rockfield. The reality of those seven months made giving up the dream a relief rather than a disappointment. As my brother Robert said, 'What are you trying to prove? That you are Arnold Schwarzenegger? I wouldn't sleep one night in this house without a gun.'

With the dilemma of holding it all together unsolved and with Alexei away at school, I accepted with gratitude the invitation from my American friends.

My United States residency had lapsed after my marriage so I was a little nervous at immigration.

'What is your purpose in coming to California?'

'I am a painter and I am coming to paint, so I hope you will give me some time.'

'Six months' said the stamp in my passport.

Kenny and Chris were loving parents to me. They found an open backed Chevrolet El Camino, which was a perfect mobile studio. I bought my first heavy duty easel and a huge beach umbrella for shade from that Mecca of all-one-ever-needs, Ace Hardware. Kenny, of course, had a selection ready of attractive straw hats. We drove around scouting and selected the first view and the following morning they waved me off.

'There she goes ... Van Gogh with tits.'

As I kicked down the big engine of my El Camino and took off with the mufflers backfiring that first morning my heart beat like a tom-tom. If this painting wasn't good these people around here will take one look and dismiss me as a local crackpot.

Cock mout kill cock

Sometimes a shot of fright is just what we need to pull the best from us. Usually the stronger the excitement the more sensitised the response so, with all that adrenalin pumping, the painting got off to a great start. In front of me in the distance was the Palisades. These small rugged mountains – with colors in a range of blues, pinks, mauves, olives and browns – change like an opal and from their base the vines in springtime shoot a fresh, pale green. After a few hours, I was lost in it and my initial self-consciousness was forgotten. A man in a big, white jeep stopped and came over to say, 'That's my vineyard you are painting.'

I nearly broke my leg hopping down from the bed of the truck to pump his hand and, gasping for breath like Doris Day, hoped that he didn't mind me working there.

'My my my, you own all, gosh, all that land in front of us here?'

'Four hundred acres.'

He turned out to be a well-known third generation vintner and that vineyard was a joke to what he owned. His modest house was a stone's throw away and he introduced me to his family immediately. Their white clapboard, nineteenth century farmhouse had a huge vegetable garden at the back and their excess was placed in a tiny stall across the street in front of the house so that people could help themselves. People in Cadillac's would pull up to my shock and help themselves. The friendliness of the people of California is so unique that one doesn't quite believe it at first. When I mentioned that I would like to paint water but the little manicured lakes with Japanese bridges and willow trees were too tame for me, he said, 'Wadder? I'll show ya wadder.'

He drove me into a fenced area with over a thousand acres of untouched wilderness. There were viewpoints from which you could see the entire Napa Valley. Little vineyards were tucked into the wild setting like jewels and there were three huge lakes full of perch, catfish and trout. There were mountains with eagle's nests in the crags, wild mushrooms and raspberries. It was breathtaking and it was private. He gave me a key so I could come and go as I liked and paint my heart out.

In wine country, where a special harmony lay in the balance of man and nature, every glass of the end product was delicious and I finally 'understood' wine. My favorite was the one Chris bought by the case with the lovely name *Far Niente*, which means 'to do nothing'. At first sip, I was transported to that eternal summer day, painted by Monet (the one of the field of wild grasses and a lady with a parasol at the top of the hill, her white dress blowing). I tasted all that.

Looking back as I am now, that six months may have been one of the happiest of my life. In the long days with sunlight until ten o'clock and the low humidity I painted as I had as a young woman, working on three a day as the light changed.

When I was tired, I relaxed with still lifes: roses; peaches; blood red tomatoes so ripe that they sat on the warm ground and corn on the cob, sweet as candy. Some mornings we would catch the Farmers' Markets, where they sliced open the nectarines for you to taste. It was impossible to resist buying a huge bag of them. There were displays of goat cheeses, home baked bread and preserves as well. I remember some beets that I was painting in the studio delaying the preparation of a roasted beet salad with goat cheese.

'Judy, aren't you finished yet? We need those beets for lunch.'

'These beets can't be eaten until they are painted. Tek it easy, tek it easy, soon come man, soon come.'

All the paintings came home for the last show at my gallery in Cross Roads. The area had become so derelict that I knew it was the end of a place that I was sentimentally attached to. It was the most successful show that I had ever had and I was moved that my buyers and friends had widened their appreciation to accept the new subject matter. This success was meaningful because it was the last exhibition in the cradle of my career, where it had all begun.

Jimmy Jobson in the seventies.

Jimmy and me.

Jimmy, 1974. The commissioned portrait that started a relationship. First exhibited in Kingston and later in New York.

Rockfield, 1977, the year I first saw it.

My father's grave face when he first saw Rockfield. He advised strongly against the purchase.

Cookie Kinkaid, me, Ken Grooms & Chris Lovell, San Francisco, 1990s.

Kenny & Chris in Jamaica.

Out of self-imposed exile, at a costume party, with Pierre Rouquairol.

Mary Hanna, the princess of my childhood.

Early days at Rockfield.

Richild Springer, my friend from Wolmer's Girls High School, who became a celebrated dancer in Paris.

My brother, Robert, opening one of my shows. My sister, Peta Gay, is between us. Spanish Court hotel, Kingston, 2013.

Summit meeting of Albert Huie & Edward Lucie-Smith, Rockfield 2000.

Inell Atkinson, dear friend, confidant and my interpreter of present day Jamaica.

Edward Lucie-Smith and me at the book launch of, *My Jamaica*, London, 2004.

With Jonathan Clark at the London Show, 2011.

Publisher, Nick Gillard, at the London Show, 2011.

Dave & Alexei,
father & son.

David Alexander Russell
& Sabrina Cesolini at
their wedding, Rockfield,
12 May 2001.

My three granddaughters: Zoe; Francesca & Sofia.

Zoe & Francesca patiently wait while Mr Chisholm strips sugar cane for them.

Alexei's women, Christmas 2017.

My family.

Working on 'My Land', as I named the painting, with my favourite painting companion, beloved Rocky the Rottweiler.

Chicken merry hawk is near

I visited the Napa Valley a few times more. In the fall to see the colors and in winter with its dark, wet days, which reminded me of Scotland. I painted indoors in the little studio beside the log house using a paraffin heater for warmth. On my last visit, I was obsessed with the heraldic form and colour of persimmons and did a series of paintings of these ancient fruit. We would throw a lunch party at the end of my stay and sell a few paintings. It might have continued like that with annual visits if Chris, the rock on which our little nest was built, had not gotten cancer. His fight for life took precedence over everything else and life changed dramatically after that.

In the year that he had chemotherapy, he managed to earn so much money for his company single handedly that they gave him a full-sized cardboard cut out of himself and an abstract oil painting, not a very good one I privately thought.

He called from a Ritz Carlton hotel somewhere, 'Hey Judy, they have given me four vacations at four Ritz Carltons. We just checked into the first one but we are so bored. We'd like to come to Jamaica instead to see you.'

'Come.'

Time moved with fireworks and trepidation into the new millennium. And for us there was a huge crack in the universe and the impossible happened. Kenny and Chris separated. In all the years I'd known them I had never heard a cruel exchange of words. Illness and the vicissitudes of life took their heavy toll but they are still friends for life. And to spend an occasional evening with them in Florida, remembering those perfect years in California – an example of American hospitality that rivaled Jamaica – is an ongoing pleasure.

The America that they showed me on my second time

around was a solace at the hardest time of my life. These friends became like brothers who took the heavy burden from off my head, just as I had seen the gardeners in my childhood lift the huge baskets of vegetables from the heads of the higglers who came to the back of the house at West Avenue.

Wha fe do?'

Suh it go.

11

Pierre

Everywhere yu jump macka juk yu

In the mid-90s, the early landscapes were dismissed by the art community as commercial work. A local critic attacked my first landscape exhibition with the venom of a snake who had been looking for an opening. This was depressing but as I had been just as uncomfortable with his former praise, I did some dismissing of my own.

If I had wanted to do commercial work it would have been a simple matter to copy photographs in the comfort of my studio where I would not have had to contend with sun, changing light, wind, rain and insects. Most people only see subject matter so there is a reflex response when a painting is of trees, sky and sea, which are generally considered pleasing. After one hasty glance they will pronounce, 'Oh beautiful,' and that would be that.

In the art world that which is praised by the majority, who need no special training, is universally condemned with the damning word 'accessible'. No distinction was seen between my work and the artistically devoid landscapes on the side-walks that share the same subject matter. Paradoxically, accessibility was precisely what I was after. I wanted my work to leap straight from my blood stream to the heart of the viewer without barriers or the need for interpretation. To be out of fashion in a tiny place that is paranoid about this was to prove an embarrassment to the provincial arbiters. My work also suggested European art schools, training and a slew of other political red flags.

However, the genuine response of the uneducated, albeit superficial, kept me going and I always worked steadily. In fact during an anxiety attack in the middle of the night shortly after Hurricane Gilbert, I counted up what I had produced for the year. It averaged out at a finished piece of work every two weeks.

Kingston had many more galleries than when I began and a thriving art market was developing. For as money loses value people look for something else to buy that will increase in value. However, the thirty-five percent gallery commission pushed the price above the threshold of most of my potential buyers, so constant economic stress added to my woes at this time.

Wata more dan flour

As often happens when we are in a low point, I had attracted a bad relationship. No he wasn't a married man but he might just as well have been. The hapless gentleman inadvertently triggered a great deal of psychic energy, which had a lot more to do with my relationships with my parents and their hopes for me than with him.

My mother's death from colon cancer had just taken place and the intense grief I felt got mixed up in my emotional state. In the year of my mother's illness, I had hardly painted a picture. Afterwards I was grateful for the redemption time, as her prolonged illness had allowed me time to show that I still loved her. The enormous loss removed, with one swipe, all the conflicted years that I had with her as an adult. There was no need to fight with her anymore. These years were replaced with my earlier childhood adoration. Her life had kept my father's life going but now they were both gone.

I had not exhibited for five years, which was unprecedented for me. Of course I was working as always but in the tunnel of my mind I was grappling with the past. The result was a deepening unhappiness and confusion, which left me filled with self-doubt and starving for affection. Affection was not this gentleman's strong point.

What start bad in de mawnin nah come good in de evelin

But at the height of my starvation Pierre entered my life and he offered a feast. It was at the exhibition of a fellow artist's work that a man, about my height, came up to me and with a strong French accent said, 'I love a painting of yours that is hanging in the back room here. I have come several times to visit it.'

It was a small portrait of Grandolph the Informer. We talked for a while and when I was moving away he pressed a card into my hand and said with intensity, 'Please call me.'

I hadn't been out much for many years and in the space of time during my long relationship with Jimmy and the tunnel that followed, I had become as reclusive as Miss Cotter.

However, I was bored and wanted to somehow reconnect socially so I kept his card.

Months later Inell and I were chatting about how dreary social life in Kingston was and I was wondering if I should have a small dinner party again as I used to when I was younger.

'Yes and invite the Frenchman.'

I asked a few people to dinner at my apartment and with my heart pounding with fright called the number on the card.

'Hello, I don't know if you remember me but we met some months ago at …'

'Who could forget you?'

When he came, Inell studied him like a scientist and reported that he had looked upset when the last man arrived. But as soon as he saw the man didn't know which way to go in the apartment he visibly relaxed. When everyone left he stayed a little longer and looked slowly at my portfolio of paintings moaning softly to himself, 'Ahhh, the sensuality, the sensuality, the sensuality.'

It made me feel completely transparent because no one had ever seen or commented on this before – the strong connection between my sexuality and painting. The truth was I could become aroused just squeezing out the paint from the tubes.

My birthday was soon after that dinner and I was invited to a party but was tired of being alone so I asked him to accompany me.

'Pierre, it's my birthday and I don't want to be alone. Would you escort me to a party that I'm invited to?'

'For me, it would be an honor.'

On the day of the party, when I drove through my gate at the entrance to the apartment grounds, the security guard came out holding a huge bouquet of flowers with a card from Pierre. He was beaming as if he had bought them for me himself. It may sound pathetic, but like a distant bell through mist, I started to remember what being treated well felt like.

Pierre was the Director of the Alliance Françoise de la Jamaïque. He was having a puzzling time in Jamaica because he was presenting French cultural performances – such as jugglers and light shows – that were being completely ignored. When I heard about the low admission fee for his events and the venues where they were staged I said, 'They are throwing those invitations into the wastepaper basket as quickly as they can get them out of the envelopes.'

'Why?'

'The tickets are too cheap and the venues are associated with do-gooding. Kingston is no different to anywhere else – the key is money and snobbery.'

'You are the only person oo tell me dees.'

'Well, if you don't want the truth don't talk to me.'

Soon after I met Françoise, an older woman, who was a great friend and compatriot of Pierre. I liked her too. She had had a radical past as a member of the Red Brigadistas. Her conversation was provocative with a liking for polemical discussion on the nonexistence of God. But she could be very funny as well. She told me that when I had called he had raced into her nearby apartment and shouted, 'She called!'

Françoise had been two years on the island but when she came out of the car at Rockfield she said, 'At last, I arrive in Jamaica.'

On that first visit, we saw Mas Joe coming from his field with a huge basket of turnips and we bought them from him. Françoise declared, 'I make turnip soup.'

Lawd

I thought how ghastly but she peeled them with great care and diced each one with every piece exactly the same size. Soon the most divine smell filled the kitchen. That soup was a revelation. She could cook like a Goddess. Afterwards, when I painted the basket with the remainder of the turnips I could still taste the sweet, earthy freshness of that soup.

Soon a cultural exchange started with food. They had been told that Jamaica had no culture and thought that our only dish was fricassee chicken and rice and peas. I introduced them to the rural food that is not considered good enough to give to foreigners: salt fish and susumber; roasted yams and breadfruit; callaloo and johnny cakes and 'turn' cornmeal.

They were fascinated and Pierre dropped the word 'susumber' into his conversation to show off how well he knew the country. Susumber grew wild at Rockfield and they loved hearing that Haitians use it for Voodoo and feared Jamaicans because we eat it. In turn they taught me the dishes that were the equivalent in their culture – the dishes that developed out of poverty, like onion soup.

They would roast a duck and serve it with green peas that tasted like lettuce. This was followed by an exquisite little apple tart – the pastry light – with the apple slices arranged just like those in glossy gourmet magazines.

Pierre sent for pâté de foie gras and truffles for me to try and attempted to teach me about wine.

'Judy Ann, do you test dee stone?'

'No. I don't taste any stone.'

'Dis wine is from the stony soil of Provence. Ok, we try another. What do you test?'

'Well, I don't know if it's my imagination but this tastes like a damp, ferny place?'

'Very good. That wine is from the forest region in France.'

Apart from food, there was another passion that made knowing Pierre fun and that was clothes. The original peacock, I never saw him in the same outfit twice and would look forward to see how he would be dressed to collect me every single time: one suit was silk in the weight of a scarf; there was a seersucker for midday and a collection of pipes and cigars and hats would complete the look.

He asked me to exhibit at the Alliance and I agreed but preferred my own long locked-up little gallery for the venue and began working again for an exhibition.

They started coming every weekend. I would work all week and they would rush into the house to see the new work. With their interest fanning it all back into life, thirty pastel drawings poured out of me like a stream that had been unblocked, in six months. I was using the most perfect, luminous pastels on earth. They were hand rolled in France. Pierre wrote to the family who make them and sent photographs of the drawings. Can you imagine how amazed I was when the Sennelier's replied with a nice letter inviting me to stop by to see them when I was next in Paris. I thought they were a brand name on a box but they were real people. I combined those soft pastels with the harder American crayons (or Conté) that could be sharpened with a Stanley cutter blade to get some crisper lines. I developed a way of cutting the fields of colour with the edge of the blade for sharp highlights. This also avoided the flabby softness that you see in a lot of pastel paintings.

We did the show in the formula that had begun when I was twenty-two. But by the end of it, I so enjoyed working with Pierre that I was open to new ideas. We planned another show immediately.

The second show was mainly landscapes. I thought that the avoidance of landscape was cowardly. I lived on a beautiful tropical island, which had a huge visual taboo – a heartbreaking sunset every single day. The reality of the island was being denied by its artists.

Pierre adored the process of painting. He would get himself an armchair, a hat for shade and his pipe in order to sit behind me and watch the painting grow. It was as if he were watching a show on television. I took him to visit a few studios, first of course being Albert Huie's. He had not exhibited in many years but with whom I was still going out into the bush sharing good painting spots. When we leave this earth, if we are lucky, we will have a long list of memories of the days that made our life worthwhile. Those days spent with Huie, that lovable big brown bear of a man, will be near the top of my list. The flowering Poinciana trees around every corner of the drive to our painting spot would make him crazy. He would be practically leaping out of the car and he would in the end get annoyed gruffly saying, 'Oh drive quickly past it.'

He couldn't take them for granted. It was as if he was seeing them for the first time. The Poui Trees in flower last just a little longer than a butterfly – three short days – so he would be in a passion during this time. The next day I would recognise them in his studio by the few strokes started on a little canvas, like a memo to return.

'You went back?'

'I had to.'

With these quick notes on location, he would finish from memory. I would work on one of mine for a month and he would produce ten in that same space of time. We never glanced at each other's work – sharing the same subject was friendship enough – but there was one piece of advice that was a huge help and I pass it on to whoever has occasion to paint water.

'You must ignore the water. You must paint everything else and its reflection as well as you can. Hold back, hold back, hold back. Do not touch the water. When you are finished, just a few quick horizontal touches of light and do not touch it again!'

I tried it as he said and it worked: the water floated.

The show that Pierre designed was called, *Albert and Judy, Two Painters, One Heart* and it was the best experience exhibiting that I had had in years.

'Suh … how you get that?'

'What?'

'Get Albert to exhibit at your gallery?'

'By simply telling him that I did not intend to touch one dollar of his money.'

I would never charge a fellow artist commission so the expenses were listed and Albert was free to contribute to them, which he did generously.

Most of the paintings that came in were sold already to his loyal fan club of collectors.

The French Ambassador opened the show and no one was invited who did not like our work. So there were no 'bad mind' people counting up the prices, exuding slitty-eyed resentment and ruining the evening for us.

'I do not want my artists upset. Anyone 'oo upset you, you tell me and I ax them to leave!'

It was good to be protected for a change.

Pierre cleared up something else for me that had caused me sadness. I told him that it distressed me how I was treated by my own Jamaican men, whose open hostility to me had grown and which he could plainly see for himself.

'They are so considerate to other women, for example following them home or calling after a party to see that they got home safely, small courtesies, but not for me. They don't treat me like a woman.'

'They are thinking, oh you don't want a man? So you must teenk you are a man. Well dees is 'ow we play, can you do eet?'

The missing piece of the puzzle – the piece that you thought you would never find – fitted into place perfectly.

Once I referred to someone as 'black' and he said, 'Why do you say 'black?'

'Because I am speaking about a black person.'

'But you are all black!'

'I didn't know that. I thought I was white when I was a child. Now I don't know what I am. I'm like a lizard that changes colour according to the agenda of who is speaking to me. I am called brown, red, and often 'a red-nayga-from St Elizabeth.'

About pricing paintings he said, 'When you buy a painting it must 'urt you a little, not so much that you can't buy it all but it must cause a little pain.'

'Why?'

'Because that is the only way you can share in the pain of the artist who painted it.'

Around this time I was still trying to get a telephone at Rockfield. I had been trying to get one for fifteen years. There was a stack of pleading letters in a thick file – unread I'm sure. Nothing had worked, although everyone else in Higgin Town had a phone but me.

One evening, out with Pierre, I saw the head of the telephone company standing near to us. I asked Pierre if he thought I should just simply ask him for a phone and he said, 'Why not?'

So I went over to this famous and powerful man and metaphorically rubbing my big toe into the ground said, 'Ah, excuse me Mr Matalon but I wonder if I may speak to you?'

'You have a problem with your phone?'

'Oh! How do you know that?'

'Because I'm seventy-seven years old and attractive women never speak to me unless they have a problem with their phone.'

'Well I don't have a phone and I've been given a novel reason why by an employee of your company. I was told that I wasn't important enough. When I asked him what would constitute importance if paying the bill on time didn't do it, I was told that I had to be a Minister of Government or the Prime Minister. Do you see my problem?'

'Can you give me the name of the person who told you that?'

'Yes, but I wouldn't want to get him in trouble.'

'But you are the official artist for the company.'

'I know. Isn't it ironic?'

It was true. I had done many paintings as covers for the phone books.

One of them, a street scene, had caused a major scandal because I had subliminally included a small bit of graffiti with the initials of the opposing political party in an election year. The party in power had threatened to recall the entire issue of phone books and Talk Radio had raged for a week with the controversy.

'Do me a favour. Put this in a letter to me.'

I went home and wrote a letter telling him how I had cried on his wife's shoulder at the hairdresser and I had offered my body to the man at the phone company's office in St Ann's Bay. '*Please* help me Mr. Matalon,' I ended.

Two months passed and nothing happened. Well, that's that I thought. I give up.

I was up at Rockfield painting a seven-foot wide triptych from the verandah. I was barefoot, covered in paint. Pierre, who had taken up painting and was pretty good at it too, was working at the other end of the verandah when Mr Matalon drove in. I thought I was hallucinating.

'How did you find my house?'

'You are a very brave woman, I picked up a boy in the area who led me here and I thought twice about that too. I've come to tell you that I cannot get you a phone and I'm sorry because you are the first person who has asked me nicely. Usually I have to put up with abuse.'

He suggested that I get a fixed cellular and offered me a contract to do ten more covers for the phone company. That would be two covers a year, for the city and the country, for five years. The fee I asked for was reasonable as I thought that I should be paying them for bringing my work into every house in Jamaica. Declining my invitation to share a sandwich for lunch, he indicated the seven-foot painting that was in progress and said, 'And when you are finished with this, I'm interested.'

He bought it for the boardroom of the telephone company and Mr Meyer Matalon became one of my heroes after that day.

My fixed cellular rarely worked though. I only got Spanish speaking operators from Cuba – which legend has it that you can see from Rockfield – and hardly ever got a call through to Kingston.

By the time Pierre left Jamaica, my damaged self-esteem had been restored and for many years I associated him with rescue. More than he knew, our friendship brought fun, laughter and *joie de vivre* back into my life and something more important, trust.

I never saw Pierre again. He remarried, lost his second wife and returned to France where he became headmaster of a school. But we have remained friends thanks to the advent of Facebook. His enthusiastic reaction to my paintings posted online invariably delights me. He had said that sometimes people were bridges to other people and that certainly turned out to be true.

12

The Huie Book

Me throw me corn, me nuh call no fowl

To work on commission is always difficult for me as it has been for a great many artists before me and it is the reason why paintings as 'jobs' cost more. The lack of inspiration makes the process less enjoyable and this can sometimes be seen in the finished work.

One of these commissions was so stressful that it stopped me accepting commissions for several years. It was a panorama of Kingston ten feet wide, requiring three vanishing points and painted on location. The view was iconic – familiar to anyone who lives in Kingston. I wanted a true portrait, a record of Kingston that everyone who lived there and shared my time could relate to. It was a killer. Working on that scale on location, made it the most difficult painting I had ever done. I stretched my own envelope almost to breaking point. It took several months – working on a platform out of doors – with the huge canvas clamped precariously to three shaky easels in dazzling light that reduced the pupils of my eyes to pinpoints. The staff at the house where I was working made my life a misery during the long work period. Not knowing where to place me socially, my paint-splattered clothes combined with my carefree manner confused them and brought out a virulent hostility.

'Who she think she is coming in here looking like that? Shi don't seem to unnerstan that I run tings in here.'

I am often asked, especially when a painting takes a long time, how I know when it's finished. In painting there is an exquisite term for that moment: 'Realisation'. If the artist's process is aborted, or not allowed to reach that moment naturally, the painting fails, which is why working on commission is so tedious. There are just too many elements that are out of control: from not being allowed to ask that the noise of the lawnmower be turned off; to the distracting household activities; including sometimes a running commentary within earshot.

'Boy look how fast they do it eh? And you know how much she want for that?' The sensitive people, the ones who watched the painting grow with fascination, could not afford to buy paintings. The ones who could afford to pay felt they had ordered a service. I was going to be paid good money for nothing really because I was born 'gifted'. Payment did nothing to make up for the lasting damage of a bad experience. I found the only way to purge it from my life was to do something from the heart – only for me.

Coincidentally, right after finishing my *tour de force* I saw a photograph of an old Rasta amongst a montage of photographs in a pictorial book about Jamaica. It was the face of Jah Wolfe, who lived in a tiny shop way up in the Blue Mountains behind Kingston. Jimmy and I had spent time with him during those days of adventure, exploring the soul of the country. I felt a pang of regret that I had never drawn that striking face at that time, but it was exactly what my own soul needed now. I drove up there immediately and rushed into his tiny shop. Over a decade had passed but he remembered me.

'I saw your face on a book Jah Wolfe and I remembered you. I feel sick that I never drew your wonderful face. Please can I come and do it now?'

We struck a deal.

'Jah Wolfe, I will pay you a modeling money. It is small but you will get it each day. It may take a long time to sell the drawing but when I do I would like to pay you the thirty-five percent that I would have to pay to a gallery because I am going to sell this drawing myself.'

'How much would that drawing sell for?'

'Probably nine or ten thousand dollars.'

He gave a deep bow.

'Then we are agreed and what is honourably embarked upon must prosper.'

Jah Wolfe's hospitality was aristocratic – whatever he had was yours. If you were his guest he shared all the treasures of his life, which, by the way, were immense. He did not see himself as poor, perhaps because he had in such abundance the things that mattered most to him.

He would say as he strode around his yard, 'All that you see here is mine.'

The treasures were green bananas and sacks of coffee beans rather than his tiny shack with light filtering through a million cracks, making the darkness inside glow with an extraordinary light. There were a large flock of chickens, a river with a little bathing pool, around which he placed on the rocks bouquets of flowers in tin cans as if it were a living room.

We worked outside in the yard and he would get up often to sell to his customers: half a soda pop bottle of cooking oil; two cigarettes or a bottle of beer; small purchases just to get through the day. The smoke from his campfire and his ganja spliff drifted across his face while I worked and the sounds of the river and the chickens made the sunny yard a cheerful place.

I borrowed some of the things he was vain about – crisp

green bananas, a huge bunch of red peas in their pods, coffee beans – and did a vanitas back in the studio, trying to recreate that illumination in his shack that seemed almost sanctified. For this painting I returned to an earlier method of starting on a raw umber ground leaving the shadows thin and building up the lights with 'impasto'. John Constable used this method for those quick preliminary oil studies, which I consider his greatest work. It works well for 'alla prima' painting outdoors. When you add the notes of dark and light there is a connecting mid tone already there so you can paint fast.

One day, in the splintered light of that little space, Jah Wolfe said, 'You won't believe this but God has stood up right here in this shop with me.'

'I believe you with ease because this is exactly the sort of place where he would be.'

I would solve the dilemma of commissions with a waiting list. If someone wanted a seascape I would say, 'The next time I do a seascape for myself, I'll let you see it first. I'll do it the size that you want but if you don't like it when it's finished, you don't have to have it. Someone else will always buy it.'

More often than not the encouragement of working in a small world where I could actually meet the people who bought the work outweighed the disadvantages.

When someone would say shyly to me, 'We have one of your paintings you know.'

'Oh do you? Which one do you have?'

'It's a small one of a Poinciana tree. We've always had it. My husband grabbed it when the roof went in the hurricane and I said why are you taking that? He said because it was the most valuable thing in the house.'

That would make a thrill race through my blood in a current of real happiness that made up for everything else.

Huie and I had become equals but I began to hear denigrating remarks about his work and sometimes they were made in the context of praising mine. I was completely repelled by this. Competitiveness among artists is ludicrous, as each person's work is unique. All I had ever aspired to was to be worthy of joining in the endless line of my fellow artists. To stand at Huie's side was enough. Turner aspired to paint as well as Claude Lorain and his dying wish was for his two greatest landscapes to hang beside his master's. Not to replace them. They hang together now at the National Gallery in London. You may like one over the other. You are free to do so but it's impossible to say which is better.

I had learned from Huie a great deal – not about how to paint, no one can teach you that, but something almost as important – on how to live as an artist in Jamaica. We were bonded through surviving some destructive attitudes to artists every one of which he had experienced before me. He was never mealy mouthed. He was a straight talker and said exactly what he thought.

When a woman invited us to attend a lecture on 'business management in art', which was to begin at eleven o'clock in the morning, he turned to me and said, 'I don't think that leaving your studio at eleven o'clock in the day when you should be painting would be proper business management, do you?'

To a young artist who said that he couldn't paint landscape from nature because he didn't have a car (this to a man who painted all over the island traveling with his wet painting on the top of a country bus) he said, 'You know what, *move* from in front of me. It makes me sick to look at you!'

Wutless!

In representational painting, which we also shared, a declaration is made. There is no place to hide. I would be complimented when he would say, pointing at a painting in an exhibition with an arm ineptly drawn, '*We* can't get away with that, can we?'

He was genuine and his work reflected that honesty. I always remember a quote from him that had nothing to do with painting. It stayed with me as it was so spiritually charged, 'I worry for people who try to harm me. I warn them not to try to harm me because they will harm themselves.'

One evening at a book launch, a local publisher said that he was interested in doing a book about my work and in the same evening the Chairman of the National Gallery asked me why I no longer sent paintings to the annual show. If I was having a hard time surviving between shows with all the help I had received, I couldn't imagine the lot of the younger painters. I said, 'If I were starting out now I don't think I would make it.'

The Chairman invited me to come to a meeting with him to explain why I said that.

When I went to the appointment I had no idea I would be facing the Praetorian Guard. It was obvious that the crowd of people around the table were in a defensive state when I mentioned the reasons why I had lost heart in 'The National Art Movement'.

I had come with a proposal that the board mount a retrospective for Albert Huie in his eightieth year. This in conjunction with a commemorative book so that the young painters of the island could see how the line in painting evolves, which is one of the ways to encourage a high standard. The very idea of being so presumptuous as to suggest things, have opinions and ask questions such as, 'How come my work has not been selected to represent Jamaica in any foreign show in fifteen years?' which is a long time in anyone's career, was so shocking, so out of order, so outrageous, that it was as if I had personally ordered the assassination of the curator.

An employee of The National Gallery answered my question in art speak.

'Representational painting is very unforgiving.'

When yu trow stone inna pig pen ah who qui qui ... ah him yu lick

I left at that point. Or rather, I left after I said that if the National Gallery could not mount a retrospective for Albert Huie, our first professional painter, it should close its doors and admit that it had failed art in this country. Privately I wondered, if they could ignore his life's work, what would be my fate? Also I was shocked to discover that in the community where I imagined I belonged, the reality was unmistakable. I wasn't good enough for this 'club'. Worse still, I did not have a friend.

Want to know who you fren is? Form like yu fool fool and lay dung a roadside

After that there was an enormous silence. Clearly there was not one morsel of food left here for the hungry sparrow hawk that had been circling a long time over that barren terrain. It was time to leave the overcooked ashes in the hearth. Time to seek live food and survive.

I thought the Huie book was still a good idea and one that I would get a good deal of personal satisfaction from doing. So I used the opportunity that had been offered for my work by the local publisher and went to see him to suggest a book about both our work, which would have an even bigger audience. It could be formatted as my homage to him, rather like the 'Two Painters, One Heart' concept. He liked the idea and I started to look for an author.

But first I got on my hotline to God.

'God please help me to do this because I have no idea how to do it. I don't have the knowledge but I know that you have already placed in my life all that I need to do it. Help me to see it.'

I had no doubt that if I could get Albert's work to any expert out there it would be recognised at a glance for exactly what it was: genuine painting from Jamaica that met international standards of quality without any need for mitigating excuses, interpretations or explanations.

As I flew away from official art in Jamaica, I had to give up the illusion of club membership. I say 'illusion' because what had I actually lost in real terms?

For years, if my work was mentioned at all in the annual show it shared a sentence with several other women artists who were in a similar state of invisibility to my own.

Leaving Fool's Paradise again was, as always, lonely. My painter friends gave me the cold shoulder and I missed the company of artists so I reached out to my old art school friends.

Johnny, from Scotland, came to visit and I told him I was searching for an author to do a book on Albert Huie. He suggested several and encouraged me in the project.

There were a few dead ends and then I read a quote in an article written by a journalist, Annie Paul, who had once written a good review of my work – one that I appreciated so much that I carried it around in my hand bag for weeks. So I called her to ask where it came from she said it was from a book by Edward Lucie-Smith. That name was on the list of suggested authors that I had so it rang a bell. Turned out I had actually been at the same dinner party with him years before in London but we had not met then.

Nutting before its time

I ordered three of Mr Lucie-Smith's books and read them. He was the right man.

I hadn't read art criticism in many years because, when one is engaged in the real thing, reading the meaningless language of the critics becomes increasingly tiresome. This language has become an art form in its own right, specialising in obscure sentences often disguising a total lack of content. Yet here, with delight, I read the clear prose of a man who was first published as a poet. I couldn't put the books down. In *Latin American Art of the 20th Century*, he assesses the work of Botero (who the art world frowns upon) and I saw that he thought for himself. If he could be fair to Botero, he would be fair to anyone. And aside from all that, he was born in Jamaica.

Brawta

I liked the symmetry of a great Jamaican painter being written about by a great Jamaican art historian and published by a great Jamaican publisher. Well, the publisher was the flaw. Not wishing to raise false hopes I hadn't mentioned my project to Huie but now I went to him and said, 'Does the name Edward Lucie-Smith mean anything to you?'

'I knew his mother.'

I took that to be a sign and wrote to Mr Lucie-Smith and invited him to come to Jamaica to assess the work of Albert Huie. I offered to take him to see the paintings that Huie considered his best work. I included some photocopies of a few paintings and a 'bio'. Months passed then I got a letter saying that he would come.

What don't happen in a year, will happen in a day

Mr Lucie-Smith had a 'window' of one week's duration in the entire year. I still had no idea in this world how I was going to pay for his ticket. In the meantime, I went to several companies to try to get the money for the project. Everyone was pleasant enough but there were more and more dead ends. Christine, who I had gone to art school with, said, 'Go to Air Jamaica, they will give you the money.'

Mr Butch Stewart was running the company at the time. As I was waiting to see his right hand woman, Betty Jo Desnoes, an office maid – just like our Miss Enid at my brother's advertising agency – offered me a cup of coffee. Once my father had seen Miss Enid dressed for going home at the end of the day and said, 'Miss Enid, I didn't know you wore glasses?' She replied, 'Yes sah but ah don't drudge in dem.'

When Air Jamaica's Miss Enid brought me the coffee it was so full of condensed milk it tasted like liquid toffee. I had a flash of psychic reassurance as I sipped it. My God. I'm going to get the money.

I went in clutching Mr. Lucie-Smith's heavy books.

'I have never begged for anything in my life but I am begging you for a ticket to send for this expert who is at the top of the art world and is willing to come here to write about Huie's work.'

She listened and at first she said nothing. Then she made one phone call and it was arranged.

'What are you going to get out of it?' My brother growled this out loud, articulating what others were thinking.

I had tried, in brief excursions, to develop property that belonged to my family with varying degrees of failure. I had worked hard on various projects right up to the point when the women's work was done – the donkeywork. The projects would then mysteriously halt right there. No phone call would be returned. I knew that was the system. At the top level it was 'penis to penis'. The Huie book would be no different; I knew that it would stall because I did not have a penis.

Huie had a friend who was like a son to him. This man was called Alvin Fong Tom. He owned the largest collection of Huie's paintings and had been collecting his work for many years. Besides that, he was a trusted advisor of the Huie family. Gaining Alvin's respect was key to the success of the project but I could see, written across his face, that same question my brother asked. I went to him and said, 'I need you to do this.'

'Why do you need me?'

'Because you have a penis and I don't. You have to be my penis when the project stalls and I need you in place from now for that moment.'

'Why can't it succeed without a penis?'

'Because then a woman would have to get the credit and that cannot be allowed.'

A word here about the remarkable women of Jamaica – if we went on strike the island would be finished in a week. As I get older, I am increasingly puzzled though by our abdication of power. We have, after all, brought up the men as expressed in the famous phrase, 'My mother who fathered me.' Why had we bred them to be irresponsible peacocks? To quote John Edgar Colwell Hearne, 'Jamaican men are permitted a degree of self-indulgence without domestic penalty, are physically pampered, get a thoroughness of attention without parallel in any other western culture even the Latin American'.

The power of the women according to Hearne comes from the emancipation of the slaves when the women controlled the food grown and sold and chose their lovers rather than wait to be pursued. He continues, 'The dominant, almost dominating position achieved by women during the slave period persists today. It operates for the most part outside the contexts of politics and commerce, almost indifferent to the power rewards these fields can give. Yet the women of Jamaica constitute an emotional ruling class and like all ruling classes they are unsentimental and acutely conscious of their power.'

That throws some light on these admirable undercover women who do the homework and can answer the questions but who, by so doing, are always being blamed for 'emasculating' the men. I think that the women of Jamaica have done their best in a 'no win' situation. Masculinity is a code that can only be handed down by men. We don't have to be cripples for men to walk. And sister, if you are afraid to be 'unfeminine' as he might punish you by withholding sex, I say get yourself another lover.

13

Meeting Mr Lucie-Smith

De olda de moon de brighter it shine

As I waited anxiously for Mr Lucie-Smith to come out at Montego Bay airport, I did not suspect for a second that I was about to meet someone who would change my life. His white skin surprised me because I was expecting a black man. He had long white hair and was wearing denim with a beautiful, jeweled belt buckle. 'Oh Thank God,' I thought when I saw this unstuffy outfit. He's nice. I said, 'Thank you for coming.'

'Thank you for asking me. I wondered why no one had asked me before.'

'I read that your hobbies were walking the dog and malice.'

'Yes but the dog died.'

He made me laugh and we were friends in that moment.

I had never been inside a Sandals hotel and was amused to find myself in resort Jamaica – such a sanitized version of island life. We sat through 'orientation' while the sound of an exercise class close by reverberated. Everyone we passed from manager to grounds man said, 'Hi, how ya doing?'

Sweaty brides in white satin hiked their wedding dresses up to get past people in bikinis. Return guests threw their arms around waitresses, who assured them that the light rain would soon stop. I stole a glance at Mr Lucie-Smith's impassive face and wondered what he was thinking.

That day he photographed some Huie paintings and, in the evening, I was included for dinner with his one remaining contact in Jamaica – a lady who belonged to the sophisticated plantocracy whose heyday was diminished if not yet gone completely.

When we were offered yet another drink before dinner, one of the party said, 'No thanks. I've had four.'

'But four is *nothing*' she declared.

It was quite an evening. Mr Lucie-Smith hadn't spoken much, as I watched anxiously some distance down the table, so I said when we were leaving, 'It's impossible to know whether you are having a good time because your face doesn't show anything.'

'I'm having a *very* good time.'

The next day we drove to Ocho Rios, where a second complimentary night for Mr Lucie-Smith had been 'arranged' – courtesy of the formidable Betty Jo Desnoes. In nearby Rockfield, I already had a house full of guests. Johnny and Joe McIntyre, both painters from Scotland and Joe's wife, Sarah, were there. On their arrival some days before, as I drove them up the hill from the coast – passing the little shops lit up at night, with the people playing dominoes in silhouette and the music blaring – there was a kind of moan in the back seat of the car from Joe.

'Oh magic, magic. Magic lanterns. Oh, I love this. *Magic*.'

So I deposited Mr Lucie-Smith in resort comfort and drove home to find domestic chaos on my hill. Guests have a difficult time without me at Rockfield and the water tanks and the stove had defeated them.

I called Alvin Fong Tom, in Kingston, who was bringing over Albert Huie and his wife for the summit meeting the next day. All the Huie collectors were also included for lunch.

'Alvin, can you believe at a time like this, the oven is on the blink.'

'I will bring a lasagna.'

'I have no *oven*.'

'I will bring it hot.'

This is why I love my Kingston people. They do not let down the show. The next day an entourage arrived with a waiter dressed in black and white to help. He gave me a wink as they swept in. He was a friend who was doubling as a waiter and he just took over in the kitchen.

After lunch the deal was struck with the three men. For clarity, it was decided that the book should be Huie's work completely. I could certainly see the sense in that too and agreed wholeheartedly. I was glad to have been the catalyst. Also the 'bad mind brigade' would have seen my inclusion as my 'piggy backing' on the great man.

That night, when everyone had left, we sat around the dining table talking about painting with Mr Lucie-Smith. I felt as if it hadn't all passed me by. I felt a part of the big family of painters in my time – part of that community that I was starving for in my jungle. Johnny knew all the contemporary painters that I had never heard of so I was glad that he was there. For me listening was more than enough. Both painters were shocked to have met this famous art historian while on holiday in Jamaica of all improbable things.

The next day we sped into Kingston to see the Huie paintings at the National Gallery and some of the bigger collections. Once again Alvin came to the rescue and put up Mr Lucie-Smith. He had a proper household, with breakfasts being served on terraces – the expected colonial lifestyle of my generation. At my apartment the fridge had absolutely nothing inside but the makings for a salad and a bottle of vodka in the freezer.

Work began in earnest. Edward or Ted, as I now called him, personally photographed all the paintings without comment. The ones for the book would be selected back in London and the chosen paintings would then have to be rounded up again and re-shot for book quality. I had a hard time keeping up with the enormous energy of the man. Every afternoon at four he would notice my exhaustion and gently say, 'Well, I think it's time to put Miss Judy back in her box.'

Gratefully I would slip away for a little rest before dinner.

It turned out that Edward had not been in Jamaica since the early seventies and had not enjoyed his visit on that occasion. He was glad to be 'home'.

It had taken three years to reach this point. Yet when the text arrived and the money was paid to the local publisher I was completely cut out of the project. I had no one but myself to blame for this. I had never had any experience in the salaried world of commercial enterprise except for the five weeks working in my own father's business. I didn't know how to flatter or watch the tone of my voice.

I had gathered the material and handed it over. There was a photograph of Huie and his wife, Phyllis, getting married – looking about fourteen years old. I wanted that placed beside a picture of them fifty years later. Phyllis had contributed so much to his success.

Instead, the pubis of a sexy nude was cut out of the painting and placed beside the younger wedding picture. I objected to the tawdry juxtaposition in no uncertain terms, 'No! Cut out pum pums anywhere in the book!'

After that it was a lucky thing that Alvin was in place to speak for me.

It was made very clear that I was not telling them how to do their business.

However, Alvin and I got only one brief look at the layout before everything went off to the printers. He knew the paintings so well that he managed to correct several that would have been reversed. And then, as I predicted, the project stalled.

The perfect text had been edited to include a startling array of changes. I called the publisher and asked to have the mistakes removed.

'Those are not mistakes. They are 'editorial decisions.'

'Well, you can call them what you like but please would you have them removed because Mr Lucie-Smith knows how to write a sentence in English.'

Silence.

'Please, I would like the book pristine with no mistakes.'

I could feel my mother's blood flowing through my veins and he, understandably, had had quite enough of this uncontrolled impertinence.

'Well, if that's what you want, Judy Ann, you will have to find another publisher.'

He had been dying to deliver it, knowing full well that there were no other publishers at the time.

I called Alvin.

'Well, they have played their ace and say that if I want the changes taken out I must get another publisher. Good thing I haven't played mine yet.'

'What is your ace?'

'Alvin, I don't have one right now but by tomorrow morning I will.'

Broken by that familiar disappointment, I cried all night.

In the morning I called Alvin and said, 'You are my ace and it is why you are here from the start. Please go down there and find out what he wants to complete this project, penis to penis.

Alvin called back to say that he wanted me to apologise. He

would withdraw the editorial decisions and I would apologize.

'Fine. Tell him I'll be happy to do that.'

When yu han is in de lion's mout, tek time draw it out

I wrote a letter apologizing for my bad manners and admitted that I didn't know how to 'handle' people, which is true. I don't. As it turned out, with this impasse over, events speeded up. The publisher proved to be a good sport, I learned to be more of a team player and Alvin saved the day.

When he called to tell me that the galley proofs were back I said, 'I'll meet you in your chapel.'

He had a dear little chapel on the grounds of his house and when he came in I was prostrate before the altar, literally. The galleys looked great, the well-known images enhanced by their newly packaged sheen. It was an exciting moment.

The flight that brought Edward back to Kingston for the launch was eight hours late. I picked him up and with some trepidation asked, 'So, how was your flight?'

'It was like the entire country in microcosm. We had sassy women in tight clothing saying, 'Is anybody serving here?'. We had people smoking ganja in the loo with the pilot announcing, 'We know who you are.' I sat behind a Rasta family who had an enormous framed portrait of Jah. We had a fashion show mid-flight and the steward opened his shirt right down to his navel on his final turn. I think that Air Jamaica is an absolutely brilliant airline.'

He recovered enough to hang personally all the paintings from the book for a retrospective at Devon House. It rained like mad that night but there was a stupendous turn out and a major traffic jam – all the hallmarks of success.

To my death I will remember the look of child like wonder on Huie's face when Edward said: 'When you spend your life in the international art world, you can get the idea sometimes that a sense of beauty has been lost and that is a rather depressing thought. How good it is to return to Jamaica and find that beauty is alive in the work of Albert Huie.'

It was all done with no money. It was done with goodwill and just in time for Huie's eightieth birthday.

Ted wrote in my copy of the book, 'For Judy Ann, without whom this certainly would not have happened!'

And when it was all over he said, 'Now I would like to spend some time with you talking about your own work.'

All this time I had not shown him any work of my own. Occasionally, when we were viewing Huie paintings, the owners would also have a painting of mine and they would point it out. He would glance at it in silence and I would want to strangle them. The reason was terror pure and simple.

I didn't sleep the night before he arrived to talk to me about my work and when I opened the door I felt like 'a poor wee timorous beastie'.

During our conversation I said that I had accepted years ago that what I was doing wasn't relevant any more and that I was sorry that skill, which I found so thrilling, was no longer appreciated and he said, 'You would be surprised.'

At the end of that talk I knew I could ask a question that took more courage than I thought I possessed.

'So, do you think you would be interested in doing a book for me?'

'Yes, I think I would.'

He also gave me some excellent advice about how to approach it.

'Start with distribution. Do not produce the books and then look for somewhere to sell them. Have the distribution worked out and then produce the book.'

I thanked him. He arranged for a wonderful painter and

good friend, Michael Leonard, to write to me about composition and took a quiet interest in my work from then on. But I don't think either of us knew that I would find a publisher. On the subject of publishers I did not have great memories but I kept that to myself.

In order to do the Huie book, I had learned how to email because that was the only way to communicate with Ted. I had also joined a club. It was called the 'Jamaica British Business Association' and it was the first organization that I had ever joined. I was standing at a cocktail party in Kingston watching a foreign man work his way through a crowd who elaborately pretended not to see him. His face grew redder as he tried to nod and smile at people who refused to see him. When he reached me I said.

'Hello'

He stopped dead and gave me a look of gratitude. He was a Scot, called Jim Malcolm, who became the British Ambassador in Panama. We chatted for a while and I told him what I was working on. He invited me to lunch at this organization that he was trying to bring to life. When I went to the lunch he introduced me to the gathering as though I was just like everyone else – not a mad artist. It was a refreshing change.

Once a month there was a lunch followed by a talk but I enjoyed them because a lot of the people who attended were British and it reminded me of Scotland. I said at one of the lunches that I would like to meet a publisher and someone replied that they would let me know when any were arriving.

In a short time I received an invitation to meet a list of publishers who were coming to the island seeking what they called 'market share'. I arrived at the British High Commission on the evening of the party dressed with care – silk evening pants and my best shoes and with my hair cut and gilded. The word 'publisher' was associated in my mind with distinguished men in suits with graying temples. Instead, what I saw was a rather lacklustre looking crowd of disheveled men and women of the rural schoolteacher type. There were some trestle tables on which were spread educational textbooks with soft covers. I was about as out of place as an elephant in the garden.

Seeing a woman in a black cocktail dress who looked a bit like me, I walked over to her and she said,

'Who are you?'

'Oh, I'm just a woman at the wrong party.'

'Oh no you're not because you've met me!'

She turned out to be the High Commissioner's wife and she was charming.

A man who was listening to our conversation asked me why I was there.

'I came because I wanted to meet a publisher but not like this.'

'What do you mean?'

'I don't want to do a textbook. I want to do a commercial book.'

'Well, you should speak to your namesake, Macmillan's. They are the commercial publishers.'

I took this to be an unmistakable sign and looked with interest at the man he indicated. And so I was introduced to Nick Gillard.

When I first saw Nick he looked younger than my son Alexei and my first question was whether he worked for someone else.

'I'm the one who commissions the books.'

Mawga cow ah bull mooma

So I launched into my pitch. I could see that Nick was interested and that interest grew when he saw my portfolio.

We made an appointment to meet in London where I would introduce him to Edward Lucie-Smith.

The meeting went well and we both listened as Ted gave us the benefit of his enormous experience. I was assured from the start that at no time would I be cut out of the creative process because they particularly wanted my input as an artist. I worked on the book in complete secrecy – under the radar of the destructive 'sus' that overwhelms so many projects before they start in Jamaica. When the contract arrived, I read the first line and it was clearly between 'The Publisher' and 'The Author'. This must be Ted, I thought. How nice of them to send it to me – probably just a courtesy. I flung it in a drawer and it lay there for three months until I got an email.

'Ms MacMillan would you sign the contract please and return it.'

I raced down to a business advisor who has become a friend to get him to wade through the legal language for me. He read it slowly and said, 'Judy, this is an honourable contract between you as the author and the publishing house.'

'But I'm not an author.'

Then catching an inscrutable look from him, I asked, 'Ok what is the difference if I'm the author or not?'

'Royalties.'

Just before Ted was to arrive to work on my own book, my car was stolen.

Aiyee sah. Bad luck worse than Obeah!

I rented a little car with no air conditioning and a hatchback that didn't stay up. It was all I could afford but what a trial it was with so many paintings to transport. The first afternoon, as I fetched and carried, he photographed seventy paintings in one go. I had never seen such professionalism.

There was not one word, no wasted energy. One whole day, of the four we had, was lost because of rain plus all the cameras he had brought jammed. Kingston sends you a day like that, every now and then – a day straight out of the 'Book of Job'. We were outside of a patty shop in Cross Roads getting lunch. Filthy water was coursing halfway up the side of the hot little car and a madwoman ranting loudly on the pavement. When I got in with the bag of patties he said, 'If only they knew'.

I knew what he meant. A book looks magical with its glossy pages but the reality of this day was as far from that as the moon.

When a book takes as long as mine did to do it is lovingly crafted. Every detail is considered. Inell was there from start to the finish and never lost interest in the minutiae. I also got to know my young publisher over several lunches at Terra Nova Hotel where he always stayed. He hated one word above all and that word was 'launch.' I learned to avoid that word because I didn't like to see him wince. There was no budget for book launches and inside his publishing world there is a superstition about planning them until the book is finished.

So I worked on the launch in London secretly.

When the date for the launch finally came near, Hurricane Ivan threatened Jamaica with extinction. The tension was terrible as it was a Category 5. 'Gilbert' had been only a three. I prayed like Martin Luther King. I prayed like Mother Theresa. Luckily, Ivan turned out to be a grumpy old man who tried to mount three times but was only able to deliver a glancing blow as he left. There is a rumour that an old Rasta stood on the south coast holding his staff aloft and rebuked Ivan rendering him unable to strike. It was Gilbert, the destructive teenager, who gave us the direct hit.

Afterwards, with just a few days to the launch, there was

still no communication and no road to the airport. A friend got her power back before mine and I raced round to her house to email London.

'Are you coming Judy? We have been so worried.'

'I'm coming if I have to rebuild the road to the airport and fly the plane myself!'

As the daughter of an advertising man, part of me could not help realising that Ivan had put the word 'Jamaica' on every computer screen around the world – with only a week before the launch of a book entitled, *My Jamaica*. You couldn't pay for marketing like that. Nick decided to thank Ivan by donating the first one thousand pounds to the Hurricane Ivan Relief fund.

When I finally held the book in my hands for the first time I cried a little. It had taken a chunk of my life and it meant so much. It was a fun party. The Jamaicans drank wine but the English people all drank rum punch – made by my sister Peta Gay in Christine's kitchen. She had used a secret ingredient (brown sugar from Jamaica) explaining that it made a huge difference to the flavour.

One of sour, two of sweet, three of strong and four of weak

My brother was suddenly proud of me and he paid for my ticket to London. He even offered to help after that major event by sharing his contacts in Kingston's business community 'A list'. This was the ultimate old boy's club (and just as importantly their wives) and it created a new respect for me, which opened previously tightly locked doors.

At the party, everyone gobbled up the cocktail patties made by a Jamaican company in London. The books sold out and there was chaotic ordering. It went on very late with people spilling out onto the pavement – all the hallmarks of success. Edward spoke, the publisher spoke and I made my first ever speech.

'For every Christmas and every birthday, I received from my father my favourite thing – a new art book. Confined to bed with chicken pox, I spent the hours trying not to scratch with Rembrandt. But having my own art book may have been beyond my dreams.'

The next party was for the launch in Kingston. Ted returned for this and hung my paintings just as he had done for Albert Huie. It was overwhelming for me to see the size of the crowd who came to Devon House that night. It seemed like everyone that I had ever met in my life was there. In the flood of affection, I began to understand how much this book was going to change my life.

I spoke again.

'I have had sixteen one-man shows since my first in1966. A great many of you here tonight were at that show. You have witnessed my baby steps, nurtured my development, seen my failures and to my great joy your children are now buying my work. I thank you for your love and support because here among *you* is where my success matters most.'

To Ted I said, 'In defining and placing me so elegantly in time, you have healed more than you know. Working with you has been an education and a delight. You have ended doubt and your respect for my work has changed my life.'

Ted made everyone laugh by opening with, 'I think that Judy Ann loves Jamaica more than she has ever loved a man.'

From then on I was treated differently. There was now a 'category' to put me in. And it was a tiny and conspicuous minority who could not bring themselves to say 'nice book'.

Grudgeful and bad mind

But the majority was happy for me. And so a new sense of 'belonging' started to smooth away the edges from my misfit persona.

Without a pause, I had to get back to work immediately as a third launch and exhibition had been planned in Miami.

Wait, yu not easy

Some years before these events, I had been to an exhibition at a gallery in Coconut Grove. I had sent some images off to them at the owner's request and she asked me to 'pop in' when I was next in Miami.

The mystical timing of events continued. A disk with all the images for the book had been sent to me the same day that I went to Coconut Grove for our meeting. An attractive woman with a slight French accent stuck the CD into the computer and shouted, 'Sachi, Sachi, Sachi! Come and see. Look at this gem, look at this gem!'

Sachi, the gallery owner, came herself to look and immediately offered me a one-man show to coincide with the launch of the book. I went home and produced sixteen new paintings, which I sent to Miami as well as ten paintings from the book.

It was a grueling amount of work. I couldn't sell anything for all the months it took to do them because they were all committed to the show. So at the time, when I was perceived as a big success with a book, I was having an even harder time financially than ever before.

If yu want good yu nose haffi run

For me the best thing about that Miami launch was the way that Ted spoke about my work. For many years, I had considered critics and what they called the 'Art Market' the enemy of the artist. Many buyers and their brokers, even if they like paintings, do not like living painters and see them as lazy uncontrollable people who are avoiding the drudgery of a salaried existence. Ted was that *rara avis* who looked at paintings with clean eyes and no preconceived ideas. Those are the eyes we paint for.

In the end I sold four paintings but I was bone tired. I had completed a long-planned project and I had been thrice launched. But I wanted to be home; with mornings at Rockfield; my solitude; cane fields in sunlight and the Poinciana in full bloom against a blue sea. Often when returning home – when I saw Jamaica from the plane again – a little tear would slip out from under my sunglasses. 'Thank God', I would whisper, for the beauty, which is my home.

However, there was no time to rest. I had to throw myself into intense work immediately because I had been included in a major exhibition at an old and prestigious London gallery, the Albemarle. It was as if all the opportunities that had passed me by were now coming in a flood. Ted was the curator and he wanted a landscape from the interior. The show posed a question, *What is Realism?* and offered a wide spectrum of completely varying aspects of realism in answer to that question. Fifty artists were included from fifty countries.

First I had to paint my entry. I knew it would take a month, minimum, so I chose a Kingston location where I could get to work easily with no wasted days. I chose a Jack's Hill view, that included an old colonial water tank, from the lawn of a friend's house in the hills behind Kingston. Her incredible panoramic view was my alternative Rockfield in Kingston.

I hadn't bargained for the famous Jack's Hill bush fires. When I returned to Jamaica to begin the painting the whole hillside had burnt. There was now tremendous colour – with dense brick-red mango trees and 'Naples Yellow' bamboos – glorious, unusual colour. The terrifying fires would come close to the house making a sound like gunfire. One day, holding a water hose so heavy that I thought it would pull me over the precipice, I fought a fire with four other women before sitting down at the easel to paint.

The fires were followed by unrelenting rain, stormy grey skies and the grass-covered slopes, to my utter despair, turned greener and greener every day – seemingly as I painted.

A 'deadline' is well named. They are killers. Paintings don't understand them and don't cooperate either. In my own process, it is helpful to leave the painting and come back to it fresh but with the deadline this wasn't possible. I know that since a canvas can be covered in paint in five minutes many people don't understand what is taking so long. I paint in layers, which are partially transparent. You can see the under-painting and I go over and over the surface – building up these layers – recording little visual 'truths'. Some stay and others are removed until a harmony steadies all these movements into a balanced network that pleases me.

To meet the deadline was stressful but I wouldn't have missed it for anything. It was a great pleasure to be included in the impressive catalogue and to see the work of the other artists, many of whom had worked as long against the tide of fashion as I had.

From early on, I had been told that everything I wanted to paint was irrelevant, already done, a pastiche of the past. *What is Realism?* Demonstrated that this type of painting still has a huge audience.

Admittedly, the show was top heavy with photo realists. But I confess that I am thankful for this movement because it has helped to keep realism alive. The death of painting has long been predicted and photography was expected to do it. I enjoy the drop dead, show-off skill of the photo realists which is almost mocking. I fancy I can hear the spirits of the ancient artists, especially the Italians who do it best, 'Oh you want photography? Well, we can do that too but can photography do what we do?'

The best part was when they closed the doors of the gallery and we realised that everybody left inside were artists. We were given a private party with champagne and sushi. I thought of Huie's stories of the colonial days in Jamaica, when he described how the artists sat in chairs under their work and were not expected to take part in the party. I could hear his braying laugh as he related the shock caused by the swirling entrance of Lady Molly Huggins, the newly arrived Governor's wife in the 1940s.

'But where is the artist? I want my picture taken with the artist!'

Aiyee sah

There was not one arrogant person in that room. We all ran around like excited children, 'Which one is yours?' Where are you from?' I was invited to so many studios – from Tuscany, Canada and Australia – and halfway through it all I recognised Ricardo Cinnalli, a painter from Argentina.

'Look, I don't mean to embarrass you but I can't believe I'm meeting you. I think your work is breathtaking.'

'Please come to my studio while you are in London. It's in Spitalfields.'

As if this were not enough the show was reviewed by the *Evening Standard* in London. Ted explained this was a miracle, as London newspapers seldom review shows held in commercial galleries. Runway space goes to official venues like the Tate. A further miracle, my painting was one of the three that were singled out for mention. According to the curator, the critic had spent a long time looking at it and in his article mentioned the sorrow of loss that permeates my work. My cup ran over.

By now, as you can imagine, Ted had become a hero to me on the level of Lenin to a communist. I kept waiting for it to stop, as it seemed too good to be true. But on it went.

I would come to the door of his little study where he lived on his computer, even dozing off in front of it for catnaps, his huge head slumped.

'Errr Ted.'

'WHAT!?' he would bark, his voice like a guillotine. I would catch my head from flying off my shoulders and, silently congratulating myself for my courage, continue, 'I was wondering if you would like a cup of coffee?'

'Oh thank you, *love* a cup of coffee, thank you.'

I understood. He lived alone like me and, like me, he had an unbroken tape in his head. He was listening to his inner voice and interruptions were actually painful.

I scrubbed his tiny kitchen until it sparkled, trying to find ways to show my love although I'm sure he saw in my eyes whenever I looked at him, my gratitude for these gifts coming into my life. I had been many times in bohemia, grubby rooms indifferent to décor. I had slept on sofas, wishing I had a cleaner sheet. But the kindness of bohemia always makes up for what it lacks in comfort.

And his books were a treasury, piles and piles of books. I devoured them hungrily – speed reading through the art of each decade, style following style, right up to my own time. I had been so busy painting that I didn't even know I was a 'Post Modernist'. I remembered in art school, just before throwing my last book of art criticism out of the window, reading about Barnett Newman and Ad Reinhard - black on black, one stripe on a field of red - and feeling as if I had walked into a wall.

Ted asked me if I was going to Cinnalli's studio and I said, 'Oh I will drop him a line thanking him but I am sadly, much too shy to go.'

Humble calf suck de most milk

When I arrived for dinner at his flat a few days later he said, 'Cinnalli is joining us, I've invited him to dinner.'

You may not find this remarkable but before he even said hello to me, he said, 'I like the way you layer the experience from day to day.'

He then proceeded to speak about my painting with complete understanding. I never knew that people could just see what I was doing before because no one had ever commented on my technique like that.

Respect is a healing thing.

I told Ted that as the years had worn on, each time I slapped a coat of white paint on the walls and put a few track lights up and invited the public to see my work, it had been with an ever- sinking heart. It was a feeling of futility that I was still just the little girl who dreamed of being an artist but that it was all in my mind only.

He had made it real.

14

The London Show

Every dawg have him day and every puss him four o'clock

The evening before the opening of my show at the Jonathan Clark Gallery in London, my art school friends, Johnny and Joe, came down on the train from Scotland. We had a curry together just like when we were young but we weren't young anymore. They were still amused about the unexpected, very Jamaican juxtaposition, of meeting Edward Lucie Smith on holiday years before. Now I had to fill them in on how the London show had come about.

Once upon a time, way back in the 1970s, a friend had invited me to a party for her grand mother in Denmark. It was a once in a lifetime experience. Her grandmother was the matriarch of a famous cheese making family. In the party was a young Englishman who had come to buy paintings from my friend's cousin Otto. Cousin Otto owned an ethereal, pale yellow castle that looked like the inspiration for the ones in Disney animated films. It had a moat, a chapel and three thousand oil paintings. The Englishman had started out in the art business very young, cleaning and restoring paintings at Christie's. Cleaning Guardi's and Canaletto's is a great way to develop your eye and Jonathan Clark has a great eye.

At the time I found his cynical attitude abrasive and his upper class accent intimidating. He seemed very arrogant.

We accompanied him to an auction where he picked up several nineteenth century paintings at reasonable prices, as he was stocking a gallery he planned to open in Los Angeles. I overheard him say, about a paltry painting of Salome holding a tray on which rested the head of John the Baptist, 'Oh I'll hire some hack to paint the head out and put a bunch of grapes or something for the American market.'

I burned with hatred in the back of the car. I was full of romantic ideals about painting at the time and I didn't understand English humour.

He prospered and some years later I went to an opening at his London gallery in Chelsea. He was dealing in dead English artists, all the ones whose work I knew from reproductions hanging on the walls of the art college: Spencer; Augustus and Gwen John; Edward Burra; Nash and Sutherland. It was the best of the best.

It has been rare for me in life to see exactly what I want. It happened with Rockfield and it happened again when I stepped into that gallery. Like Joan of Arc, I heard a voice in my head and it said, 'This is what I want.'

Whenever I went to London after that I would visit the gallery and the standard of painting was always high and the stories of how he acquired them fascinating to me.

The Chelsea gallery was a perfect venue geographically for a book launch and I knew that the summer is a slow time when it might be possible to rent it for one night. But at what cost, I wondered. Although I had been a whole month in London, when I took all the material for the book to hand over to the publisher, I had not had a chance to speak to Jonathan even once. The day before leaving I called, 'Can you talk now, Jonathan?'

'No, I'm up to my eyeballs.'

'May I email you what it's about?'

He gave me an email address and I got to an Internet cafe and wrote my request.

That may have taken thirty minutes. I instantly got a bounce back message that said, 'This is an automatic responder. I will never read your message.'

What? He had just given me the address, I felt as if he had slapped me.

I called our mutual friend to say goodbye and said, 'My God, Elsebeth, I feel like Jonathan has slapped me man. He is so rude it's terrifying. Even his automatic responder sounds just like him.'

'Oh Judy, I don't know what happened but leave it to me.'

About two weeks after I was home, I got a call from Jamaica Inn, a famous hotel in Ocho Rios. Jonathan Clark wanted to speak to me.

'Hi Jonathan, I'm glad you called me. Why don't you and Victoria (his wife) come up for lunch?'

'Thanks Judy, we are *dying* for a plate of honest food. We are so sick of this German chef parading around in his whites and giving us shit to eat!'

'Well, that's about all I can give you Jonathan.'

I gave them instructions how to find me and went down to the village and picked up Muffy who is a woman as confident about her cooking as anyone I've ever met.

'Muffy, I want you to cook a meal that is going to sweet the life out of an Englishman. Do the pork with the ginger and the pimento and roast a breadfruit and do the callaloo. I want to taste the coconut in the rice and peas. I want it to sweet dem, girl, don't let me down!'

'Give dem brandy, Miss Judy. English people love brandy.'

'No Muffy, we are going to give them your freshly squeezed passion fruit juice.'

When Jonathan walked in he was very taken with an oil sketch that I had just finished. I was testing it by living with it for a while. It was of the current gardener picking ackees with a stick.

'Love that, Judy, I had no idea you were such a good painter. The thing reeks Jamaica.'

When I told him over lunch that I had no gallery, no dealer and that I had put on every exhibition for myself he said, 'Oh how plucky!'

When he was on his second helping of Muffy's delicious country cooking I said, 'I'm glad you are here because I wanted to ask you if I could rent your gallery for one night for the launch of a book next summer.'

'Oh Judy, I'll *give* you the place!'

My art school friends knew what this night meant to me. They too had looked wistfully through the glass windows of the galleries that symbolised success. I needed their friendship and loved them for their support but it could not wipe out the perennial anxiety that nothing would sell on the evening. Would I stand there in my good shoes, with my hair nicely combed, smiling gamely while nothing sold? It had happened before.

I got my hair done and took a taxi to the gallery. Worrying was actually all I had to do. The gallery did everything else.

'It's nothing, Judy.'

'Nothing', was how Jonathan referred to the exquisite invitation, the perfectly modulated lighting and the crisp white wine. My painting, which he had named, *Wilderness,* was placed in the window. My heart skipped a beat when I saw it there. To me it meant all those hard, hot days driving to that same spot at the side of the road up in the hills. At one point I had to move down the road a little when an attempt was made by residents in the area to make what I was looking at more beautiful. They planted huge flowering shrubs to block out the bushy hillside, which incomprehensibly to them I was painting. That one had been a long struggle. Not the work – never the work itself – but the heat, the changes and the sudden gusts of wind. One of them whipped the painting right off the easel and down into the valley below. It was rescued by a dear little man with very few teeth. He climbed down and came back up with it covered in insects and triumphantly grinning.

'But why yu don't jus tek a picture? Buy a camera, nuh man?'

In the first five minutes before the rooms filled with people, a couple, whom I had first met in Jamaica, bought *Miss Cooper* – a portrait of a standing figure wearing a maid's uniform, holding a tray with a cup and saucer. They told me that they had come especially from Kent to buy it the moment they saw it on the invitation.

To my mind *Miss Cooper* was the best painting I had done in years but it would never have sold at home. Jamaican collectors rarely buy portraits. They saw 'the people' as 'the problem' and when they ascended to their luxurious houses after work, the last thing they wanted to see on the walls was one of 'those people'. They enjoyed portraits as decorative abstractions of flat shapes but not realistically painted. Not with faces that you could look into, not with eyes that looked back at you.

It's always more satisfying selling what you consider the best you can do.

Miss Cooper had marked a return to portraiture. It had started badly because I was bored with going back to what I already knew. So I had turned the bad start to the wall and began reading a biography of Goya by Robert Hughes, illustrated with many of his famous portraits. There were no harsh white walls behind the figures and no strong implacable sunlight. Looking at the portraits again was like a refresher course. The secret of their power was in the atmospheric light of an earlier time – before electricity and before cameras. They were human beings in the living gaze of a fellow human being, a communion of souls.

Excited by that discovery, I blocked all the light in my studio. I got a rickety, old spotlight and placed my model in its glow. She sprang to life as if on a stage, amplified. I shook a little as I re-painted. My model's collaboration helped, as Miss Cooper adored her sittings or I should say, 'standings'. When offered a break she would say,

'Yu gwan. G'wan paint. I am an old soldier.'

She swayed as I played the music of her youth: 'Goodnight Irene'; 'Save the last dance for me' and 'Paper moon'. Towards the end of a great many sessions, she started to reminisce about her childhood. Without emotion she spoke of being 'given away' to a relative because she was so pretty and with light brown skin. She mentioned many times her husband who had left her 'in a board house' but 'found me in a concrete house' when he came back years later. However, her bitterness prevented her from sharing the spoils of her struggle. When he returned, she happily lived alone in her old age, in peaceful splendour, full of pride at her own achievement.

When I heard the stories about her past I knew that the painting was good because when she looked at it, she saw her life. I sold others that night but selling *Miss Cooper* was the high point for me.

Homecomings were increasingly pleasurable the older

I became. Coming back to Jamaica after that show in London was blissful. Home was a warm breeze caressing me through open windows and the smell of a breadfruit roasting on a fire in the yard. Home was the comfort of my own house and the freedom to leave a coffee mug in the sink and a book on the table. Freedom was picking flowers from the garden for every room and a little salad of tender green shoots – happy for the insect holes in their dark green leaves, the black earth on their roots. Happiness was oranges and tangerines from trees I had watched grow, sucking their intense juice while standing barefoot in the back garden.

'Now go home, become a national treasure and develop a reputation for being somewhat recalcitrant.'

That had been Ted's advice. Certainly after these events, life changed at home.

The acceptance from people who now felt they knew me was certainly preferable to those embarrassed eyes quickly averted from the paint all over my clothes. I didn't turn suddenly and catch that little sideways shake of the head behind my back, which mimed, 'She mad you know.' The patronising question 'Still doing de painting?' was replaced with, 'I'd love to own one of your paintings.'

New buyers found me, disembodied collectors on the Internet, whom I never met. Some of them were expatriate Jamaicans, whose own nostalgia for the island was mirrored in my work – images of loss but images also of so much that still remained. Older collectors now validated in their early purchases were proud of owning a piece of my work. They took them out from under the bed or the back of the cupboard and reframed them or wanted them restored. By any standard it was success so I should have been happy. So why was this physical pain always with me?

Wanti wanti cyah get ee, getti getti nuh want ee

A wise friend who is a healer came to visit. She is a proponent of the medicine of the future, which believes that pain is caused by emotions that are trapped in the body. I told her about the mysterious pain that I still had months after coming home from that pinnacle of a show in London.

'I could understand having tension before the event but I have done it. I'm supposed to be happy now.'

She said, 'That is not your pain. That is your mother's pain and you must learn to separate your pain from your mothers.'

A shocked gasp came out of my mouth. Instinctively, I recognised the truth; a truth so deep as to be primeval; a truth that my very cells remembered. I hurriedly left the room.

Upstairs, I lay on my bed and wept for my mother. I wept for the potential that she had not reached, not in my estimation but in her own. I wept for her trap, as she perceived it, the trap shared by many women of her generation. She chose comfort, protection and loss of freedom. I wept for her choice, as I know she had wept for mine. Was I still the little girl distressed by my mother's tears, determined to make it all up to her? Had this intention really driven my whole life?

Hush … de more yu look de less yu see

I did the little movements my healer recommended, not exercises exactly, just slight movements that I apparently did in my crib back in the time before scar tissue – before the catalogue of these wounds had begun. In a week the pain was gone but understanding our pathology is not enough, what to do about it is the hard part.

Without a new goal, I slowed down, painting less and day dreaming more. Although I felt justified in being unfocused for a while, as time went on, life slowly settled into the torpid island pace that I had resisted most of my life. I no longer read the local news, cared even less about the opinions of others, especially opinions that differed from my own.

My sister who was busy with her own family had been pretty indifferent to my work for years, tried her hand at painting. One day on a rare visit to Rockfield with her young son, Dylan, she was painting a flower study in my studio.

'That's really good Peta Gay.'

Dylan was indignant at what sounded to him like faint praise.

'Good? It's great!' he declared.

She joined an art class and became a passionate student. After that she had nothing but respect for what I did.

Dave was gone. He died prematurely from heart failure in nearby Florida. A hundred times I'd visited Miami and he was always there at the airport to meet me.

He had asked me just before he died, 'Have I ever let you down?'

'Not even once.'

There will always be unfinished business between us because the pain in my heart when I think of him is always there.

Increasingly, my book was used as a catalogue.

'I want one like that but can you put some fretwork in it?'

There is a foretaste of mortality in that. The wild sparrow hawk in me resisted, even resented the idea of working to order from a book, which displayed my past.

Conscious of the danger of becoming a brand name – and we have all seen the stale uninspired work of the 'important' artist – I took commissions. And as orders for seascapes became for me what Poinciana trees had been for Huie, I fought the numbing of my senses. Sometimes, when I got into the rhythm, I actually enjoyed them. I had become a professional and pride in that replaced the lost days of rapture.

On a deeper level, my solitude became a faithful lover and a constant companion. I recognised acquaintances late, like a missed beat after I had already passed them in the supermarket. I missed the company of men but passively. I didn't miss the conversations with the flying plates. I went to bed earlier and looked forward to the end of each day. I couldn't wait to get my bra off, longed for my old friends and became nostalgic for the good old days. It was as if the good times were all behind me and, although I was feeling abandoned by the past, I spent far too much time back there. It felt like boredom but it was actually depression.

Ebryday bucket go ah well one day de battam mus drap out

A fancy of mine is that my existence is like a board game for children, a brightly coloured one like snakes and ladders. The yellow sun with rays, the mountains and the sea, are represented in a naive style. The game involves moving around the board to get rid of an imp who is on the board from the start. The moves are made according to chance – a roll of the dice as in backgammon but it is not entirely random. The imp on the board looks like an emoji of a particularly malevolent gardener who had once worked for me in the country. It is a flaw right at the core of my sanctuary. The object of the game is to get rid of the imp. But no matter how hard I try, strategise or rearrange, the imp pops up somewhere else on the board, grinning.

'Watch me now! Heh heh heh.'

The pull of the charismatic serpent is always there in the garden. He is entitled because he was there from the beginning. Don't try to meet his eyes. He knows you but he will not acknowledge you. He has an historic collection of masks. He is comfortable with his power, even seductive and he has to be continuously resisted. Unaware that I was withdrawing from life again, I crept closer to his dark residence as if pulled by a magnetic force. Ennui deepened to apathy until I found myself at the very entrance of a strangely alluring place. It looks like a place to rest at last but it is really the place for giving up. A trauma slapped me hard away from it.

Surrounded by poor people I had been robbed all my life. The theft of my mother's jewelry had hurt enormously but the new robbery was even more grievous because they stole my life's blood.

Mawga dawg will tun roun' and bite yu!

Eight paintings were taken of the few that I had kept for myself, including my radiant Poinciana tree by Huie. I had swapped two of my early landscapes for the Huie and it had hung on the same wall for over thirty years, only coming off for hurricanes.

The thieves entered my open house during Mr Chisholm's afternoon nap. They hid inside and left by simply opening a door after he had locked up the house for the night. The real loss, as you can imagine, was of my peace of mind. As the months passed, I gave up hope of ever getting them back and I became afraid at Rockfield for the first time since Hurricane Gilbert. Irrationally, I couldn't shake the thought that the intruders were hiding inside the house somewhere.

Saviour Divine, what a judgment

I slept with the TV on so I couldn't hear the sounds of them coming up the stairs to my room. If my sanctuary couldn't be the way it had been before, like a spoiled child, I didn't want it anymore. I even thought of selling the house. When I whispered this blasphemy to Inell she said, 'Don't be silly, Judy, Rockfield can't be sold. Rockfield must be given.'

But there are many good things about getting older and

one of them is that whenever there is a trauma, I know now to wait. Eventually the life-giving change will appear, peeping from behind the fearful death mask that, dances just in front of it. Just wait. Pay attention while you wait. The solution could be simple and, like a pebble dropping into a pool, the answer came. If I was going to keep Rockfield, then I must change the way I lived there. It was as simple as that.

So I worked for a year on the house, which had become, during the time I had avoided it, even more dilapidated than usual. Instead of asking myself why bother since I am the only one here, I threw myself into making long deferred repairs. My plan was to have art retreats, which I hoped would open up my life and bring into it kindred spirits. Working towards this goal brought my natural optimism back and with it renewed energy. I was so busy that I forgot to be depressed and, as so often happens, creating change brought many more changes into my life. It was around this time that my granddaughters came to live with me.

15

My Three Granddaughters

Tek sleep mark death

A year before Francesca, my eleven-year old grand daughter came to live with me, a conversation with my family over dinner changed how I saw myself. Sabrina, my daughter-in-law and my son Alexei, now lived in Ocho Rios, a little resort town on the North Coast of Jamaica with their three young daughters. Sabrina said, 'You know Judy, Francesca (who is the oldest of the girls) will be finishing prep school soon and she will need to come into Kingston to go to High School. Her father wants her to go to the same high school where he went.'

'Yes and I have been waiting for this from when she was born.'

I had been deeply worried about the girls' education ever since going to a school concert some time before at the prep school in Ocho Rios. A group of eight year olds had gotten up on a stage the size of my coffee table, looking like brightly coloured grasshoppers. The music, an appalling cacophony, started and on the first note the kids rocked their pelvises like improbable little fertility goddesses to some screaming lyrics. I recall the phrase 'Control it gal!', frenziedly repeated over and over. Before the end of this performance I rose to my feet and announced, 'I'm leaving now and I am never coming back to this place.'

Sabrina laughed weakly, as what else could she do? There was no other school for the children to go to. In her soft Italian accent she said, 'They say eet is, Cul cha,' Judy.'

'They can call it what they like but I see nothing less than child abuse and I refuse to witness anymore today.'

I did go back once more to a theatrical performance of Francesca's for which she won a gold medal. She got on to the stage and bellowed at the top of her lungs an oration by Bob Marley which began, 'Africa unite, unite, unite for the benefit of your people!'

The stirring words were followed by a wild dance during which she leapt into the air – higher and higher – to the loud beat of the drums. Our nine-year-old diva was in a long white dress trimmed in red, green and gold (the Rasta colours) with her long tangled hair escaping from a knitted tam. In fact she galvanised the audience with this culturally impeccable performance. Impressed as I was, I still counted the minutes until Francesca would need to come into Kingston to High School.'

'But Judy, we can't ask you to have her live with you in Kingston.'

'And why can't you ask me?'

'Because of your work, your exhibitions …' she trailed off.

Let's face it, I am certainly not standard Grandmother material but my youth had vanished. My middle age had merged into it somewhere down the line and that too had now disappeared. It was an appalling turn of events for a baby boomer. I had smiled kindly in my youth at old ladies who fished out photographs of their grandchildren from their wallets to show me – those banal little faces that meant nothing to me. I was certain that I would never be like them. My own grandmother who smelled of lavender and was as shapeless as a barn door was what the word 'Grandma' meant to me. I had an indelible memory of being bathed by her in a bathroom that I tried to reproduce years later at Rockfield.

In my memory, I am four years old and I am standing on a cork bathmat beside my grandma's big white tub. A gas heater on the wall above the tub has little dancing blue flames. The room is completely undecorated. It is a room where one goes to get clean. She has washed me gently with Pears soap and patted me dry with huge white towels. There is a final dusting of talcum powder, on a big soft powder puff, that smells of foreign flowers: lilac; lily of the valley and violets. I feel loved and safe and that feeling is my reality.

With my ex-art school style and punk rock hair I couldn't be that 'Grandma' but I could be a sort of tropical Auntie Mame. She was the subject of a favourite book of mine that I read in the '50s. She was a New York socialite who wore turbans and smoked cigarettes in a long, jeweled holder. We got to know her through the nine-year old eyes of her nephew, Patrick, who she always addressed as 'my little love'. An orphan, Patrick came to live with her at 3 Beekman Place, New York. He wrote hilariously about his many zany experiences with this unconventional guardian.

I thought, if the people I love most in the whole world can't ask me to do what is perfectly natural because of my work, clearly my work had taken up much too much space in my life already. A small shift took place in my mind. There was now something more important, more valuable than my work.

'Francesca will come to Kingston, go to High School and live with me. My work will have to look out for itself.'

I began renovating a guest room in my shabby old house in Kingston. Years before I lived there, this house was a sort of extra house in the family, used at various times by my son, after he came home from College or rented out at times. But quite often it lay neglected and unused. Unable to cope with the constant break-ins, invited by an uninhabited house in

Kingston, I had blocked up a doorway and given the back bedroom, with attached bathroom and a small back verandah, to a caretaker to live on the premises. The years of accumulated grime, grew and grew when those rooms, long vacated by the caretaker, were no longer occupied. My grand daughter's eyes also grew round when she was told that the pile of dirt and dereliction behind the reopened doorway was going to be her room. Zoe, who always followed two years after her pioneer sister, had developed a 'wait and see' attitude and a tendency to keep her own council. But I could see that she was also appalled by this inauspicious start and relieved it wasn't her turn yet.

'You wait until I'm finished with it', I said blithely, just like Auntie Mame, and waved my imaginary cigarette holder.

My daughter-in-law is a modern Italian girl. She likes sleek, contemporary design and the latest fashion. When she saw these abandoned rooms she was silent as the grave. This restraint is one of my favourite things about her.

It pains me to remember the zigzag waves of workmen: the carpenters and plumbers destroying the pristine work of the tiler; culminating in a Jackson Pollack painter who splashed a liberal splatter of paint over all at the end with a flourish. However, two sets of workmen and one minor nervous breakdown later, when Auntie Mame took briefly to her bed, the little suite was transformed and ready – just in time for our mutual adventure to begin.

Francesca chose from a website a snazzy coverlet for her new bed and above it I had a large poster-sized photograph of her in riding clothes – splendidly seated on a horse she was learning to ride. Her most beloved stuffed teddy bear was placed on the bed and some personal treasures came in from Ocho Rios to make the room her own. The first morning I peeked in.

'Oh my God' I thought, 'I have a child. Her things are everywhere. She is here.'

The first day of school is called 'orientation day' at the Hillel Academy. After a year of preparing Francesca, quite often with Zoe, her younger sister listening with particular interest, a few photos for posterity were taken and we accompanied her to the new school. Compared with the tiny school she knew in Ocho Rios, which did not boast even one blade of grass, it must have looked quite daunting with its expansive well-kempt campus, pretty gardens and fruit trees.

Surrounded by a navy and white gaggle of strangers, Francesca looked very official in that new school uniform of navy blue skirt and crisp white blouse as she drifted away from us – Mama, Papa, and me, anxious 'Nonna'. There was a blank stare of sheer terror on her face.

That evening my little family and I had a ghastly dinner together in a restaurant and then her parents drove away. There was a cataclysmic melt down.

Even after all the conversations to prepare her, there was a tidal wave of tears. She didn't want to hurt my feelings as she got into my bed and I hugged her but she couldn't stop crying.

'Its not against you, Nonna. It's not you, but I can't do this!'

The next day, as I anxiously watched her enter the school from my car, a little girl her age flew to her side, flung her arm around her shoulders and Francesca ran off to her new life without a backward wave.

At home, food was the first big challenge. If you think you are a good cook, try cooking for an eleven year old. She seemed to eat nothing but chewing gum and a hideous cereal called 'Froot Loops'. At the end of a week, refusing just about everything, her mother came into town where she found, and removed, a huge bag of candy from her room. *Busted*.

I knew discussions about food took place in Ocho Rios at the weekend with Mama because on arrival back in Kingston the following week Francesca said, 'Nonna, would you get me some cow? I love cow.'

'Do you mean steak?'

I bought some filet tenderloin and watched as she beat the meat flat as paper. I had never seen filet treated quite so harshly before. She was dead sure that I couldn't cook and she did it herself, reducing it to a thin piece of dry cardboard and declaring it to be 'delicious'.

Foods that passed muster were on a very short list but at least she never seemed to get bored with them. Steaks and chicken breasts were all pounded as thin as paper. Foods were eaten separately and in a completely pure and unadulterated state: bread or rice without butter and macaroni without the packaged cheese sauce that comes with it. Salad always followed the meal and never varied – cucumbers, olives, carrots, lettuce and no dressing and no tomatoes. Unlike most kids there were no snack foods either, not even potato crisps and the other things kids usually love.

'Have to watch my weight, Nonna.'

'Do you like shrimp, Francesca?'

'I like it crisp on the outside and soft inside. I don't like soggy shrimp.'

I tried a tempura batter, while she watched silently exuding skepticism.

'Good Nonna. Really good.'

I added shrimp tempura to my growing repertoire of 'How to Please a Picky Eater' and made a mental note to get a stainless steel nonstick frying pan from Williams Sonoma and a turban for my hair. I was going to be doing quite a lot of frying in the evenings.

'Does everything have to be dry and crispy?'

'*Yes*, Nonna. Crispiness makes the zing in every dish.'

'Well when you go home this weekend, I'm going to have a nice bowl of gungo peas – the first ones of the season.'

'Ugh.'

'They will be cooked in coconut milk in a divine, soggy gumbo and poured over rice.'

'Ugh! Well, what's nice with gungo peas is pepper. So put some crispy red pepper flakes and some crispy plantain slices and some crispy bacon on it, Nonna. That will give it some *zing*.'

She could be right, my little gourmet.

That first term we fell quickly into a routine. I would drive her to school very early, just as I had done with her father. Like him, she preferred to be there while the mist was still rising up off the ground and the leaf blowers were getting the school grounds ready for the day. It suited me as well because I could be back home for my coffee before the morning traffic started its slow crawl on the pot-holed streets.

She played a tape of the same song every morning in the car, until we both knew every word of it.

'Well I've heard there was a secret chord
That David played and it pleased the Lord
But you don't really care for music, do you?
Well it goes like this:
The fourth, the fifth, the minor fall and the major lift
The baffled king composing Hallelujah
Hallelujah
Hallelujah
Hallelujah
Hallelujah.'

In the afternoon, she would be dropped back by a driver, so that I wouldn't have to get on the road at the worst time of the day for the dreaded Kingston traffic. This refusal to do the afternoon run – and one other nightmare drive to her riding classes at a polo ground on the outskirts of the town – were the only duties that I balked at.

In the afternoons, when I heard the gate bell I would always go to the front door to watch her walk across the lawn, her tangled pony tail lit up in the sunlight. I would whisper to God, 'Thanks for sending Francesca to live with me.'

I hadn't been aware of being lonely. I was used to my solitary life and had confided to her during the year of preparation time before she came that I had misgivings.

'Darling, I'm a little nervous about you coming to live with me in town.'

'Why Nonna?'

'Well I live a very quiet life you know. I'm worried that you won't like it.'

'Nonna, have you ever seen me watching TV? I'm *very* quiet.'

Reassurance from her became the norm as from the start she became *my* parent. This tendency was familiar from when she was just a baby and came to visit me at Rockfield. On one of those occasions when she said she was hungry, I lazily got up from resting with her on my bed to go downstairs to the kitchen. I was wearing a loose caftan and nothing else.

'Nonna! You don't wear panties?'

'Yes darling but I don't need one now, I'm only going downstairs to fix you something to eat.'

'Nonna, that is *bad*. We wear panties!'

'Oh darling I don't have lots of pretty panties like you do.'

'My Mama will buy them for you!'

Now that she was living with me, I kept my tongue in my

cheek most of the time as Francesca, my fierce little Mama, looked after me rather than the other way around.

At first I was overwhelmed by the change and couldn't work.

'What did you do while I was at school, Nonna?'

'I waited for you to come home.'

My weekends were free. I would go to Rockfield, reluctant to miss even one weekend as the time there was now severely limited by the 'school on Monday' deadlines. This was in many ways a replay. Having two houses, as well as a career and a child in school, while balancing on a painter's financial shoestring was a familiar pattern and a lot easier the second time around.

On Sundays, I would collect her in Ocho Rios, which was an hours drive away on the coast below and drive back into Kingston with her. Our conversations in the car became a good way to get to know her.

'Take the highway, Nonna, it's much faster.'

To everyone's excitement, a new highway was being built in Jamaica by the Chinese and it made the back and forth over the mountains – between the North Coast and the South – where the capital is, a lot easier.

'The highway? No darling, I can't. Nonna has never driven on the highway and I'm scared.'

Her eyes were huge in disbelief.

'But, Nonna, what can happen to you? I'm sitting right here beside you!'

I tucked my tongue back in my cheek, its new residence, and keeping a serious face said, 'Oh please, don't make me do it darling.'

'*Yes*, Nonna,' she insisted, 'I'm going to help you. You *must* face your fear.'

Later, I overheard her reporting to our shared Mama on the phone.

'Mama, Nonna was afraid to drive on the highway and I made her do it. I made her face her fear and she did it!'

Occasionally, she came into town on her own, traveling on a big air-conditioned bus. Waiting to collect her at the bus terminal, I could see in her busy walk as she came off the bus, that she felt like a big girl traveling alone. I had premonitions, in a flash, of the independent young miss that she would soon evolve into. But not yet, I thought, please not yet. This special time, just before that inevitable step into adulthood, was luminous.

Once she came off the bus carrying a little cooler full of pizza dough erupting alarmingly.

'Quickly, drive home, Nonna. I'll ask Mama what to do.'

A hurried phone call and then, 'Mama says to punch it down.'

She completed the pizza expertly and I must say it was delicious.

As a treat sometimes we would go for dinner at an Italian restaurant owned by her mother's best friend, Alessandra. As soon as we came in they would know exactly what we wanted because she always ordered the same thing: a margherita pizza to share and a glass of Sangiovese wine for me. On our first visit, the waiter noticed that I had brought a little sprig of basil from home and after that he always brought one out for me with a significant glance. We would sit in silence enjoying the crisp dough and the lovely melting cheese – so much better than our delivered ones on Sunday nights.

I told our phone-call-away-Mama, 'If I didn't know you before, I know you now because of the way your daughter behaves in my house. She is a joy.'

Francesca was unspoilt and better than that, she was conscious of it. Her father had explained, during that year of preparation for High School, that one of the few disadvantages of going there was that the children came from the affluent upper class of Jamaica and they took privilege for granted. I knew she was unsurprised and unimpressed by their attitudes. She told me that a girl her age in the car bringing her home was showing off a very expensive mobile phone. The driver had asked the girl how much she paid for it and she said that, of course, she didn't buy it herself. When she got out, leaving Francesca and the driver alone in the car, he remarked companionably as if they were allies, 'That's how dem toppenaris pickney stay.'

Francesca approved.

'I was so proud of him, Nonna because he saw right through her.'

She was also refreshingly innocent of any tendency to 'keep up with the Joneses'.

Next door to our old house, was a shining mansion in which lived a family headed by a world weary Lebanese. Her first week they spotted her through the hedge that separated our properties and said. 'Oh is that your grand daughter? She is the same age as our kids. Would she like to come over and play?'

'Yes, I'd like to' said Francesca, 'but I can't come now. Nonna and I are stuffing up a rat hole.'

Sometime later he very kindly said to her over the fence, 'Darling, keep this phone number beside your bed. If you hear anything at all in the night that frightens you, call me. Uncle Marcus will fire off his gun immediately.'

Francesca saved up her money all year to buy her presents at Christmas and was clever at budgeting in the supermarket. I was bored to coma with the supermarket so I delighted in staying in the car and sending her in to shop for dinner.

'Nonna, I got two carrots and some pasta. You don't need to get the angel hair it's too expensive and this one is just as good. I got juice, some chick-en (pronounced Italian style with emphasis on the last syllable) and a healthy snack for you.'

The planning of dinner during the drive to school every morning and the preparation of dinner every night become the major event of my day. We were both interested in the cooking shows on TV so technique was carefully discussed.

'I'm going to try it again and smash the potatoes right after they are baked so they will be more crispy. Let me smash them. Please can I smash them?'

She was not so keen, of course, on washing up.

'I want you to wash up tonight.'

'No, I don't want to.'

'Neither do I darling, just leave them.'

I went to my room and listened with amusement to the shocked silence in response to this that emanated from the kitchen. One has to be able to interpret a huge variety of silences with children. This particular, puzzled silence was familiar to me from the days of bringing up her father. In choosing my battles, I would often surprise him by not reacting to things.

A few minutes later, she called from the kitchen, 'Nonna, I'm washing up *my* dishes.'

'OK, my sweet.'

A few more minutes later, 'Nonna, I washed up everything.'

'Oh great, darling, thank you.'

She reminded me of someone I used to know myself at that age. And as the days followed each other, each one pretty much the same as the one before, I relived my youth. It was like having a living memo in the house, from the days before aches and pains, to be as good-natured as she was. If I got grumpy at an intersection on the road with the bombardment of beggars, windshield wipers and sellers crowding around the car, she would say, after a worried glance at my miserable face,

'It's always best, Nonna, to look on the bright side.'

The utter naivety of this advice would disarm my annoyance and make me smile again.

She had been rude to me only once in the first week – a mistake that had been instantly corrected by her father when I reported it to him.

'Alexei, have a word with Francesca. Explain to her that if I never put up with any damn rudeness from you, I'm hardly likely to take any from her.'

He spoke to her at the weekend.

'Franci, do you like your new life in Kingston and going to High School?'

'Yes Papa.'

'Well, it depends on you getting on with Nonna.'

This glimpse into my son's parenting style could have come straight out of the pages of Balthazar Gracian's, *The Art of Worldly Wisdom*. The lesson in expediency was effective because she was never rude to me again.

One han wash de other

On the last day of the term, she tidied her room carefully and packed for the holidays at home. I overheard her saying to herself as she looked around the room, 'I can't believe this is happening. I feel so empty.'

Soon enough her rigid diet started to expand. The first sign of this was after the holidays. It seemed discussions had taken place at home. On our long drives into town, when she opened up and spoke about her inner life, the conversations usually started with food.

'Nonna, I like whole wheat bread and porridge, cornmeal porridge with banana and I like pork chops.'

'What?'

I knew that Alexei never touched pork even at Christmas.

'Yes, Nonna. Papa makes cornmeal porridge for me and I like it.'

'Who are you? Where is Francesca? What have you done with her?

'Its true, Nonna.'

Cornmeal, I vaguely remembered with a sinking heart involved quite a lot of laborious stirring.

'I like yam. Usain Bolt eats a lot of yam.'

'Now I will crash this car. Well, I can certainly get these new items for you, I'm not sure though how to make cornmeal porridge.'

'I will show you, it's easy.'

A little anxiety had appeared about growing up, literally getting taller. Worry about one's physical appearance is a forerunner but following close behind usually is its spiritual partner – new fears from that huge well of private anxieties.

She went on, 'Nonna, I am turning into a girl and I don't like it.'

'But you are a girl, what on earth do you mean?'

'No, I am a tomboy. I always play with the boys and show them my muscles and I'm stronger than them. And I don't like wearing dresses.'

'So don't wear dresses although I must say you look very nice in them.'

'I do want to wear high heel shoes.'

'You have your own style darling and don't worry, the very best girls are tomboys and boys like them very much because they feel comfortable with them.'

After that we spoke of other things and she sang all the words to my CD of '40s songs all the way to Kingston.

'Francesca I wish you wouldn't stare at that machine when we are driving to school in the mornings.'

'Its a fabulous game Nonna.'

'Yes I'm sure, but it's the only time I have to talk to you all day and I miss that.

Can't you play it when you are alone waiting for school to start?'

She reluctantly put it away. Hoping to entertain her with the passing scene through the windows of the car, which I used to do continuously with her father, I said, 'Those cascading blooms over there are called Ebony. They know when it's going to rain and bloom to announce the event.'

She received this information in interested silence and then said quite pleasantly, 'Cool.'

Several mornings after that she asked a wonderful question.

'What are the trees thinking, Nonna?'

'I don't think that they are thinking, in the way that we do but they are recording time. If you cut down a big tree, and I hope you never do, the rings show everything that has happened to them during their lives – all the hurricanes and weather changes are recorded.

The most important thing they do is change carbon dioxide into oxygen so they breathe for the world. And they also attract rainfall.

'So we need them and they need us.'

'We need them a great deal more than they need us.'

By the time that Zoe joined us, I thought that the only thing that could be better than one granddaughter would be two granddaughters. Yet when I had first met Zoe, I thought she didn't like me. Twelve years before, when she was born, she would be brought up to the house on Sundays. She was a completely round infant – a collection of circles with the blank expression of a Fernando Botero painting. She would fasten her eyes on me in a fixed stare and she never returned my smile. It was a little unnerving. On her first birthday I rushed into their house clutching my tawdry present. It has always amazed me how angelic beings could be made so happy by the cheap piece of brightly coloured plastic that I found it an embarrassment to give them. She was sitting in her high chair when I came in and she said, '*My* birthday, not Franci's.'

My heart broke right open. Her older sister's dynamic personality was already fully formed by the time Zoe was one year old. I understood in that moment the vulnerability of every second child on earth. At about four years old, a loose tooth of Zoe's came out one weekend while they were visiting me and she wanted to put it under her pillow due to some arrangement with the tooth fairy. Francesca declared, 'Look there is no tooth fairy and you know what? There is no Santa either.'

I thought this was a little hard of her, blasting through Zoe's illusions just because she was a little older, so before the tears welled up I came to Zoe's defence.

'Well, that may be true but you have to believe in the tooth fairy and Santa anyway.'

'Why?'

'Because if you don't you will grow up thinking that only things you can see are real and that means you will grow up without any imagination.'

There was a deep silence as they both considered this and then Francesca made her ruling decisively.

'It's true Nonna because in Italy, there is a mouse, that brings money for the poor and I have seen the mouse.'

Franci, the tomboy, was always impatient with her younger sister's extreme femininity. Zoe could not have enough frills on her clothes – she adored every Disney princess – and dreamed of having a prince, of being a wife and mother. She was the target victim of the toy designers with an endless collection of Barbie dolls. I remember playing with dolls at her age too but she had a collection of Barbie dolls so large that it was cause of concern for the family because as the years passed, Zoe didn't seem to outgrow them.

One summer I said to her, 'Now when Franci goes to Italy to see your other grandmother, Nonna Antonietta, we are going to spend some time together alone and I want to paint a portrait of you in your pink dress. You will have to sit very still.'

I never had better cooperation from a child so young. She was only seven that summer but she didn't move or complain. I saw in her enormous lidded eyes and in her unsmiling face, a huge inarticulate love for me. It was a serious, steadfast love as Zoe is the lover of our family – the eternal feminine. I can confidently predict that she will be adored because she accepts herself completely. She never strives. Rather she sits on her pedestal, without anxiety and wears her tiara without a shred of self-doubt – serene as a Madonna.

Just before the portrait was finished, it was stolen along with the others in that traumatic robbery at Rockfield.

'But why do the bad men want a picture of me, Nonna?'

Bad men have been stealing Madonnas for years I thought grimly.

I didn't have the heart to start another and in what seemed like minutes, the little pink dress was too small. The wave of time drowned the moment and moved on.

Repeating the previous pattern, a room was prepared for Zoe with a huge picture of her lit up by the candles of the cake from her last birthday party. She looked like a Georges de la Tour in that picture. It was framed and placed over her bed.

There was no meltdown when her parents left, just a slow roll of huge tears running down that impassive face. Those tears were to continue whenever her parents would leave. Every single time.

After her very first shower in our shared bathroom, I saw a pile of clothes scattered on the floor. Wet towels were everywhere. I let out a piercing scream and they both came running.

'What is it, Nonna?'

I screamed again pointing a tremulous finger at the clothes.

'What is that? What is that on my bathroom floor? I'm shaking. Oh God, I'm shaking.'

They fell about with laughter and she never did it again.

Although the girls were quite different in personality in one thing they were alike.

Zoe had just as rigid a list of foods that she did not eat. Unfortunately for me, it was a different list to Francesca's. The look of intense worry on Zoe's face those first weeks were caused, apart from homesickness, by the mournful certainty that she would starve to death.

I fought Zoe's homesickness, dinner by dinner, and slowly won her over. Soon I had her enjoying real macaroni and cheese instead of the packaged kind, which was a breakthrough. So she was appointed 'Food and Beverage Manager' and chose the menu every morning. Her taste for expensive imported snack items, which she added to my shopping list in clear unhurried handwriting, incensed our 'Bursar' – her big sister. When she spotted frozen pizza rolls, she would raise her voice and stamp her feet.

Zoe made no attempt to compete with her vibrant sister. Franci was always rushing out to ride horses, play football – to be the best at everything she tried. Zoe would stay home quite *contenta*, placidly dreaming. At the end of her final year at prep school, Zoe's daydreams became reality and she played the starring role in the school play. Her part was Ariel the Mermaid and she was a natural on stage. We were not surprised. We knew that in her imagination she had been Ariel for years.

Her circles lengthened into ovals. Long legs developed and she let us know that she was going to be a dancer, treating us to performances before dinner. It seemed feasible. I could see her onstage twirling her skirt to the music.

'Hurry, hurry, hurry girls, I want you to come to dinner with Nonna's friend at her hotel. She wants to meet you and I want you to look your best so *off* with the shorts. Don't you have dresses? And do not order the most expensive thing on the menu.'

But the pure in heart take completely literally the instruction to choose whatever you would like. When the big menu was passed to Zoe, who was always sure that the present meal maybe her last one on earth, she said decisively 'I'll have the lobster and a strawberry daiquiri.'

I saw our hostess hide a smile.

During the hours after the school drop-off and preparing the evening meal, there was time enough from my duties as a grandmother to grapple with my new identity. Who was that stout rather stern person I glimpsed passing in the mirror. Where was 'The Painter'? Why wasn't she painting?

When in doubt do a self-portrait. A self-portrait is always an absorbing task. My technique, accumulated over the years, was less helpful than you might imagine. There was more to discard to arrive at truth. I had a huge introspective struggle with this one. As Oscar Wilde said, 'It is Art and Art alone that reveals us to ourselves.'

Every day the girls came in from school and they would go first to the studio to check the progress of the painting.

'Does it look like me?'

'Ah, err, not really Nonna. It's a little like you but …'

Zoe would say nothing at all but her silence was loud and cautious with a touch of alarm.

I spent many months on that painting. There were long gaps between sessions with the canvas turned to the wall. This was so that my eyes could forget the image in order to see afresh but after many months when I asked Francesca again, 'Does it look like me?'

'Yes, Nonna, it is exactly like you.'

I knew it was true because she had never lied before. I lifted the brush and it was finished.

One evening, as I railed against my frying fate in the kitchen, Franci said that she hated school and didn't want to go back and furthermore wanted to be transferred to another school as quickly as possible. While I was trying to compute this alarmingly abrupt change she asked me for some help, which I concluded meant with homework.

'If A is equal to B and doesn't like C …'

'Algebra? I told you I simply can't help with math homework. Call your father.'

'It's not Algebra, Nonna.'

In a warning tone of voice Zoe said, 'This is very important to Franci, Nonna.'

I left the kitchen and joined them at the dining table. Francesca had a large sheet of paper on which she had made a chart.

If E doesn't like C and sits beside D.'

'Wait a minute, are these people? Do they have names?'

Reluctantly a name or two was mumbled.

'Well, I'll tell you exactly how to deal with that.'

In a calm voice, I gave advice from the deep vault of my experience. I masked completely my true feelings, which were that I would cheerfully have broken the legs of the odious child who had hurt my Franci. This would have spooked the moment of intimacy. Zoe listened deeply, storing it up for when it was her turn in that particular situation. The next day when they came back from school Francesca's face was happy again. I never asked for details but I would have missed that important moment had it not been for Zoe.

If it's a truism that grandparents are closer allies with their grandchildren then that cliché was certainly true of us. I was told the things that would not be told to parents because grandmothers instinctively know how to receive information without making a big deal out of it. A big deal is what young people dread the most.

Feeding and transporting were valuable services but it was for these moments when we are needed that grandmothers are put in the world.

'Nonna! We have been in a car accident!'

There it was, the nightmare.

Love was a package deal, which came with so many involuntary flashing fantasies of disasters – a mental horror film of fear that I had absolutely no control over. My heart had shattered into a million pieces and was lying on the floor. My steady voice surprised me.

'Where are you?'

'We are alright. We are at the corner where the pharmacy is.'

'Don't move a muscle. I'm coming right now.'

The relief washed over me. And there they stood, quite intact, in the worried crowd at the corner. And as I drove them home I heard the story from their two viewpoints. Zoe's sombre assessment, 'That driver is going to get us killed.'

Francesca's excited.

'I've always wanted to be in a car accident, Nonna.'

I couldn't speak. I was silently thanking God. I was thanking Him for this reprieve.

Easter term, summer term and Christmas holidays.

Time longer dan rope

The sameness of the school routine created an illusion. An illusion that time was slow and steady, that nothing was changing. That same route every morning: the familiar potholes to avoid; the gate bell ringing in the afternoon and breaded chicken for dinner. The two girls, lit up in the afternoon sun, coming across the lawn, chatting and laughing, their legs just a little bit longer each term.

They were back to school after a special summer holiday. They had been to Europe with their parents. There were ecstatic photos: handstands in front of the Louvre; 'selfies' crowding around the *Mona Lisa*; eating crepes with Nutella and strawberries; macaroons in Paris and posing at the Prado in Madrid.

I was sitting on the shore of an immense lake. I was looking across the water, that lengthened and deepened. It was the pool of their expanding lives that soon I would know nothing about. Francesca was no longer the excited little girl – dressed for her field trip in skinny pink jeans, a turquoise golf shirt and lavender sneakers – who couldn't wait to tell me all about it. She had become a focused young woman, doing homework in her room or looking seriously at the paintings in the exhibitions we visited and choosing her favourites. She had opinions about the way they were done.

'I like how the artist left out those big parts of the picture and painted them white. I've never seen anything like that.'

The excited little girl had gone.

By now they were quite often expertly cooking dinner for themselves. I would have a second cocktail while watching the news.

'How long have you been with me now, Franci? Three years?'

'Much longer than that Nonna. This is my fifth year.'

'You have changed.'

'I promised you I wouldn't change.'

'I know, darling. You are supposed to change. It's a very long time. We have all been waiting for you to turn into a monster like all teenagers are supposed to do.'

'But don't you get tired of the same dishes all the time? Chicken, breaded chicken, chicken ... let's try something different tonight?

'What about calamari?' said Francesca.

Of course, I knew Sofia, my third granddaughter, as an infant but as she grew I saw her only on special occasions. She was quite indifferent to me and very much in her own world when I came into her territory in Ocho Rios. She was usually caught up in games or watching shows on TV in the big playroom down stairs. At two she would run excitedly to meet me. At four she would give me a hurried kiss and then at six, a lazy wave from the sofa, hardly looking up from her endlessly enthralling iPad. I didn't know her very well so during the holidays I made time to spend a whole morning alone with her. I could always entice her with the promise of animals so I was disappointed when at first she declined my invitation to come to Rockfield to see some peafowl that I had recently acquired. Hiding my disappointment I accepted her decision, saying in a mild tone, 'Come whenever you can.'

She changed her mind and decided to come right that moment. I drove up the green tunnel of the country road from the coast, which got even greener as we climbed. She played on her brightly coloured iPad beside me. On this drive, Francesca and Zoe used to love looking for the Venus flytraps and got into a state of excitement whenever we found one. Unknown to Sofia, I had an agenda. I wanted to seduce her to spend the morning as I used to do with her older sisters, in the real experience of nature. I was sure I could make that more interesting than the abstract experiences on her little machine.

I spotted an abandoned bird's nest in a low branch over the road and stopped the car. But it was too high for us to reach. Luckily, the very first man who came along down the road was someone I knew. He was the man in a roadside stall that I often bought breadfruit from on the way home. Breadfruit is a starchy vegetable brought to Jamaica to feed the slaves originally. Slave food is delicious when you are free and the smell of breadfruit roasting on a wood fire is for me the smell of Jamaica.

He got the nest for us easily with one precise chop of his machete. Right where we stopped there was a little 'lean-to' made of a few bamboo stalks.

'What a lovely house for us, Sofia.'

'Nonna, that house is very mashed up and doesn't have a roof!'

'Yes but it would be very cool and airy without a roof. It doesn't have any furniture either but we could get a chair for you and one for me.'

'There is no space for a bed.'

'We could always get all the animals from your house and make a bed out of the two chairs. Certainly we would have to fit in the tiger. He would definitely have to come.'

She had shown me her large collection of toy animals in her bed at home and how she always made space for the tiger. I was enjoying the sweetly puzzled look in her eyes as we had this conversation and could plainly see her thoughts. Is she serious or is she just saying these things? I had seen that weighing look before in her father's eyes at the same age.

When we got to Rockfield, she went immediately to see the birds and to photograph them with her iPad. Her pictures were good and, at one point to improve them even more, she got right inside the big cage with the peafowl. It looked like a scene from *Alice in Wonderland*.

Later she found a small bunch of guineps in the fridge. These are slippery, tangy berries rather like lychees but more to a child's taste.

'I hope you are ok with me having these,' she said, 'I love guineps because they take so long to eat and they're *so* good.'

'Oh yes, there are a few chocolates in there too.'

Guineps, chocolates and a slice of pizza – a perfect kid's meal.

We hunted for and found some 'shame me lady' weeds. These are a form of groundcover with tiny leaves that shrink and close up when touched – opening again in a second or two. She called them 'Shy lady'.

We made small boats out of curvy leaves, to float on one of the rainwater tanks, and decorated our boats with flowers. We picked off some dead flower heads and scattered the seeds in the flowerbeds.

Time slowed to a child's unhurried pace. At her pace, existence filled time: there was time to look at the light and shadow in the garden; time to feel the warm breeze and time for my consciousness to expand.

There is such an affinity between the very young and the old. Everything that I had learned in life, my granddaughters already knew. People get muddled along the way. We get complicated somewhere between seven and seventy. But right then in that moment a cape of calm acceptance enveloped me and erased everything that didn't matter – all those pesky little torments, anxieties and fears.

As I sat beside her on the bench, a tiny spot in my heart, a little unhealed area of anguish was soothed. She forgot her iPad in the kitchen as we roamed about and then after a long while, her mood shifted and she said she would like to go home. As we went to the car she clutched two guineps on a tiny stalk.

'Why don't you finish those off?'

'I'm taking them for Zoe.'

I thought of my own father who couldn't eat a whole mango without saving a cheek of it in the hope that one of us – his busy adult children – would come by to share it with him. Sometimes the cheek of the mango would be way past its prime by the time one of us came by. But he just couldn't enjoy it all by himself.

'Oh, don't worry we'll buy some more on the way home.'

I got a big bunch and she broke a small bunch for herself from the big one.

'No they are all for you.'

''Nonna, you are so nice!'

Forgiven. I felt forgiven. The morning had melted like butter in the sun. She smiled and waved when I left her and my heart was light. But I didn't know until later the significance of that morning. I didn't know that something deeply buried within me was rising up to the surface from my subconscious. Sofia's beatific effect lingered for a long time. I found myself smiling whenever I thought of her.

What was the quality that emanated from her? Simply that she had never known anything but love and she accepted it as naturally as her next breath. Could I dip the rag in turpentine and wipe clean an area from the big painting of my life that didn't work? Could I learn from my little granddaughter what I once knew? Not how to love – I already knew that – but how to be loved, to receive it naturally as my birthright without making a big deal out of it.

Epilogue

Jack Spanier seh, him nuh cry for Feather, him cry for Life, for where there is Life, Feather can grow

I am driving into the light.

I started before dawn, as it will be a two-hour drive today to get to work. As the sky lightens I can tell that as usual, after heavy rains, the morning will be luminous: the goats climbing up a huge pile of garbage; the derelict buildings; the ramshackle towns; the dark silhouettes of the people. Everything will be gilded in the clean-washed air.

My eyes are raking, scanning, storing and squandering images that won't be made into pictures. Rather they go into the huge storeroom filled with visual food – the living food that nourishes me.

If Huie were here he would enjoy, at first sight in the distance, the top of that perfectly conical mountain he loved. His face would light up as if he was seeing the face of a great friend across a room. The contour line is immutable but the colour is always new, as each day is unique.

'I love the morning light. When I was young I would be painting already, it's the best light of the day. Do you know what my favourite thing to paint is?'

'Flowering trees?'

'No. It's the line of light around moving figures in the distance.'

'Yes, I love that too.'

I will do it for you. I will squint into the light when you are gone.

This morning the mountains are a pale grey blue.

If Colin were here he would say, 'Ultramarine with a touch of raw umber, dear, and lots of white.'

'What about the greens?'

'Terre verte, dear, and Naples yellow. Glaze in umber to warm it, ultramarine to cool it. A drop of white in the glaze will give it body.'

I gaze for a while at a group of people sitting in the back of a little truck in front of me. The back of the truck is a stage set for their tableau, a tonal 'chiaroscuro', composed by a tropical Caravaggio. The theatrical lighting describes the volume of the woman's breast and outlines the sculptured shape of the boy's arm. As if they can feel the admiration in my gaze they wave and smile when the truck turns off.

Gone.

I remember another one of these soap bubbles that got away, never to be painted.

I was stuck behind a truck that was climbing a steep mountain hugging the bank. On the other side, a precipice fell down to death itself. A tarpaulin wrapped the top and the sides of the truck and a fold in the tarpaulin formed a deep hammock that looked like stone drapery in the strong sunlight. In this fold a boy lay cradled on the sheer vertical drop. His upturned face was chiseled in dark marble and one perfect arm lay along the top of his nest and one perfect foot protruded. He was so relaxed in this death-defying perch that he had fallen asleep.

I'm passing the once proud, new factory that Dave had come to Jamaica to build. It's in ruins, a pragmatic ghost in rusting zinc. At a fording the road is blocked.

Road wash wey, Mummy. Rain.

Turning back, I take an unfamiliar detour, which seems to be continuous potholes that are more like staggered trenches.

In compensation, grand new vistas open up before me like a huge slide show and suddenly in the middle of nowhere, there is a surprise of an eighteenth century tower. Its distinctive stonework is unmistakable – an earlier ruin in a place of layered ruins, lost dreams.

The road flirts with the sea, sometimes it peeks, just a slice of blue in the distance and now, around a corner, it leaps out and runs along the edge of the road laughing, its broad cerulean face flashing white.

I am both a witness and a guest as I drive through this fertile, chaotic mix of animals, children, cars and buildings – all in strong discordant colour. The roadside stalls are spread with coconuts, seaweed, honey, molasses and mangoes. A familiar feeling of gratitude fills my heart for these sights, these smells, and these textures. I can feel the memories running through my blood from the start of my life to this moment in one unbroken line. It's as if the slight membrane over beauty that exists in other places is torn off here.

Suh, what change? Yu still doing the painting? Yu still in yu paint up clothes and yu Barabas sandal!

At the hill, where I am working, the caretaker has opened the gate for me. He makes me as comfortable as he can: helping to carry my heavy paint basket; getting a rock to weigh down the easel in the wind and offering a glass of water when it gets really hot. Quietly behind me, he watches the progress of the painting, fascinated, like a child watching a magic trick. His genuine appreciation means more to me than the convoluted language of a critic, who will never know or come to love a painting of mine.

The sunlit view is spectacular. A little school is loud with activity. The colonial church links the scene to the past. The eternal sea – impossibly blue – breaks into pure white as it crashes silently on the distant coastline. In the foreground are breadfruit, mango and coconut trees with glossy leaves that glisten in the dazzling sunlight of this postcard perfect day.

In deep shade, under a huge almond tree, Lilliputian figures can just be made out and against these darks, pale pink hibiscus blossoms dance in a tangle of wild grasses.

Sometimes transformation looks pretty much as it did before.

My painting goes well as the reservoir of emotions that have filled my heart overflow to the canvas. After several hours my concentration slips and I begin to notice my aching back and my blurred vision. I am empty. It is time to stop for the day.

On the drive back the familiar weariness and slight depression, combine with the strong smell of turpentine and wet oil paint from my painting.

When did dreams become memories?

Hush. Ah suh life stay

I stop for a water coconut at a stall beside the sea. I ache in every limb and my mouth is as dry as sand. The owner of the stall chooses one with care. Slashing at it with his machete, he expertly prepares it for me to drink and hands it to me with a smile. It tastes so fresh. The juice dissolves into my cells with an intravenous power.

The day has cooled. Without a whisper, a window in my mind opens. I glimpse the very nature of my life and why I am here. I understand that I must live in time, never in reaction to it. My past, trapped in memory, is a colourless sheet of graph paper. It is a static abstraction compared to this intense reality, this living baroque vision in front of my eyes right now. Life must be drained without resistance, just as I put back my head and drain this fruit. The pain of it must be swallowed too, not strained out from the rest.

When my mother was dying she said, 'Judy, if you miss your time you never get it again.'

'What time?'

'The time that is for you.'

I understand now. This is my time to drink. I won't waste a drop of it. I must bring, to each newborn day, amnesia to the accumulated scars – the losses, hurts, betrayals, regrets. The only pathology of life comes from drinking that polluted water. I will be receptive to change, as trusting as a blank canvas, clean of the past, with its fearful graveyard of dead experience.

When I was young I was afraid of giving up painting. I was afraid that life's expediencies would squeeze out the thing that made me happiest. I was afraid that I would look back in bitterness because I hadn't tried hard enough to live my dream. I was always surprised when people used the word 'gift'. The struggle to do it didn't feel like a gift most of the time. To live by ones painting is to walk the tightrope of paradox. You cannot paint without money but to be a good artist you must not paint for money. Most often my destiny felt like a curse rather than a gift.

Wha fe do? Suh it go

We spend so much of our lives making the best of the consequences of earlier choices, doubting often whether those choices were the right ones. To be sure that the dreams of youth were worth the struggle to hold on to them is a transforming awareness.

We hear over and over again about the sacrifices that must be made, the prices that must be paid, the disciplining of self in order to succeed. And it's all true.

But there is something else that is true.

At this stage of my life, I am still painting not because I'm in the trap of habit but simply for the love of it. I know that one day the paintbrush will drop out of my hand but if I had never sold a painting, I would still have done it because it helped me to appreciate the extraordinary gift of life and life's beauty.

Glossary

There isn't a Jamaican anywhere in the world who will need this glossary but we are an hospitable people so I include it for those readers who are neither 'born ya' (born here) nor part of our multi-coloured, disparate and delightfully dysfunctional family. Much more than how we look it is how we talk that makes us Jamaican. However, the vernacular keeps changing so a phrase like, 'Galang yu ways, all you know to do is perplex woman daughter!' from the mouth of a market woman to a street boy may not be as common as in my childhood. But we are all bilingual from birth and whether we speak our language or not we can all understand it.

If yuh born fe hang, yuh cyan drown / Whatever is your destiny, it will be fulfilled.

Barbecues / Terraces with a dual purpose, for sun drying of crops such as pimento (all spice) and as catchments for rain water

Rock stone ah river bottom nuh know sun hot / What you haven't experienced you know nothing about

Solomon Gundy / A spicy relish made from dried herring and eaten on crackers

Pick up saltfish / A pickled condiment made from flaked dried codfish and eaten on crackers

Massa hawse, massa grass / Everything belongs to the master

Facety bad / Imperious, arrogant

Shi likkle but shi tallawah / She is small in stature but very strong and fearless

Donkey sey dis world no level, hill and gully yah so, hill and gully dey so / The world is unfair

You suck salt troo a wooden spoon / Life is impossibly hard

Duppies / Spirits

Not every thing good fe hear, good fe talk / You shouldn't repeat everything you hear

Duppy know who fe frighten / Bullies pick the easy victims to intimidate

Dawg nyam you supper / If you aren't careful, you will lose what you have

Learn fi dance a yaad before yu dance abraad / Try perfecting a skill in private before displaying it in public

Tidey fi me tomorrow fi yu / Your turn will come

Parson christen him own pickney first / Charity begins at home

Virayga / Virago

Story come to bump / The crux of the matter

Still wata run deep / A calm personality is deceptively wise and thoughtful

Gawn off / Crazy

Play fool fe ketch wise / Pretend to be stupid to deceive others

Cousin boil good soup / Harmonious ingredients go well together

Wild hog inna him coco / The mayhem that arises from a wild hog getting into and destroying a neatly planted patch of cocoa which is a kind of yam

Ah ram goat dat / He is like a male goat

Cockie, buddy, willie / All terms for a small penis.

Hood / Term for a very large penis.

Babylon must fall / Babylon refers to the establishment or the ruling class

Cawchee / A conch shell

Madda / Mother

Serious ting / An important matter

Young bud nuh know storm / The innocent have never experienced hardship

Peenie wallies / Fireflies or lightning bugs

Man a yard / The master of the house

Come see mi and come live wid mi is two different things / Appearances are deceptive. Get to know people well before inviting them to live with you.

Mannersarable / To have good manners

What nuh dead nuh tek it throw wey / Don't give up hope while you are still alive

Bumbo claat. Ras claat. Pussy claat. Blood hole. Blood seed. Pussy hole / All terms of abuse

Yu red an yu Mawger / You are a half breed and very thin and unnourished looking

Nuh mek yu right han know what yu lef han is doing / Keep your secrets even from those close to you

Gwey / Go away

Good friend better than pocket money / Friendship is worth more than money

Tun yu han mek fashion / Make the best out of what you have

Batty man / A homosexual

One one cocoa fill basket / Be patient. Do not expect success overnight

Higglers / Food sellers

Everywhere yu jump macka juk yu / Sometimes there is no respite from misfortune

Wata more dan flour / When there is not enough to eat

What start bad in the mawnin nah come good in de evening / If something starts out badly, it will not end well

Susumber / Also known as gully bean commonly grows wild on abandoned lands, backyards and in gullies.

Cock mout kill cock / Our words can come back to haunt us

Chicken merry, hawk near / Even in the happiest times, we must watch out for danger

Wutless / No good or worthless

Me throw me corn, me nuh call no fowl / My actions say who I am better than my words

When you throw a stone inna pigpen ah who qui qui ah him you lick / The person who reacts most strongly to a general non-accusatory statement is most likely the guilty party or the one most offended by it

Want to know who you fren is? Form like you drunk and lay dung a road-side / When you have no power the hypocrisy of people, even of friends, is revealed

Brawta / An unexpected bonus or reward for a purchase

De olda de moon de brighter it shine / Expertise improves with lots of practice

When yu han is in the lion's mouth, tek time draw it out / Be careful how you extricate yourself from a bad situation

Mawga cow ah bull mooma / An unimposing looking person could be closely related to someone very powerful

Bad luck worse dan Obeah / Some misfortunes are worse than a bad spell

Jugu-jugu / Not in good shape

Grudgeful and bad mind / Resentful and malicious

If you want good yu nose haffi run / To succeed you have to push yourself as hard as you can

Humble calf suck de most milk / If you do not exalt yourself others will exalt you

Every dawg have him day and every puss him four o'clock / Everyone gets a chance at success. Your day will come

Wanti wanti cyah get ee, getti getti nuh want ee / Many of the things we take for granted are luxuries to others

Every day bucket go ah well one day battam mus fall out / Constant risk-taking leads to trouble eventually

Mawga dawg will turn round an bite you / Often the very ones you have been kind to are the most ungrateful.

Tek sleep mark death / Learn from similar situations

Toppenaris pickney / upperclass children

One han wash de odder / One good turn deserves another

Time longer dan rope / Time is the master

Guineps / A fruit

Jack Spanier seh, him nuh cry for Feather, him cry for Life, for where there is Life, Feather can grow / Jack Spanier refers to a bald chicken who has lost all his feathers but remains hopeful that they will grow back. So don't grievefor unimportant things while there is life there is hope

Chronology

3 December 1945: Judy Ann MacMillan born, Kingston, Jamaica. Father: Dudley G. MacMillan. Mother: Vida J. MacMillan (née Fullerton). Grows up in West Ave, Constant Spring. Attends Wolmer's High School For Girls.

1960: Visits the Museum of Modern Art, New York and decides to become an artist.

1961: Accepted at the Duncan of Jordanstone College of Art and Design, Dundee, Scotland. Studies Fine Art (1962–1966). Graduates with a Diploma in Art.

1966: Returns home to Jamaica and teaches at The Queen's High School for Girls, Kingston for two years. Followed by a brief stint at MacMillan Advertising Ltd.

September 1968: First one-man show at the State Gallery, Kingston, Jamaica.

April 1969: Marries David Julian Russell. Moves to Akron, Ohio, USA. (Divorces, 1971).

2 February 1970: Son, David Alexander Russell, born, Akron, Ohio, USA.

1971: Returns to Jamaica and resumes painting career. Accepts a Government commission for a portrait of Sir Donald Sangster. Other important commissions include Sir Phillip Sherlock, Chancellor of the University of the West Indies.

1974: Exhibition at State Gallery. 'Raz Dizzi' purchased by Maurice Facey, Chairman of the Board of the National Gallery of Jamaica, and presented to the Gallery on permanent loan.

1977: Produces portfolio of six reproductions in a folder called 'Faces of Jamaica'. Presents one to Sir Florizel Glasspole, The Governor General of Jamaica.

1981: Buys Rockfield, a country house in the parish of St Ann, in order to develop her landscape painting.

1982: First Landscape show, State Gallery, Kingston, Jamaica.

1985: Major exhibition at The Pegasus Hotel, Kingston, entitled: 'In the spirit of '85'. Opened by The Governor General, Sir Florizel Glasspole.

1986: Participates in 'Caribbean Focus Now' Exhibition at The Commonwealth Institute, London, UK.

1988: Hurricane Gilbert severely damages Rockfield precipitating a change of artistic direction. MacMillan stops painting portraits for a few years.

1993: Exhibition with Cadien & Pearson, Georgi Gallery, Berkeley California, USA.

1994: Two Exhibitions at State Gallery, Kingston: 'Pastel drawings' and 'Two Painters, One Heart' (with Albert Huie). Both exhibitions in association with the French Embassy, Kingston, Jamaica.

1997: Exhibition: 'Paintings from the Napa Valley', State Gallery, Kingston, Jamaica. This is the last show to take place at MacMillan's gallery in Cross Roads.

2000: Co-edits and produces the book 'Albert Huie: The Father of Jamaican Painting' (Ian Randle Publishers Ltd). Collaborates with Edward Lucie-Smith who writes introductory essay. Launches at Devon House, Kingston, with an accompanying exhibition of paintings from the book.

2004: 'My Jamaica: The paintings of Judy Ann MacMillan' with an introduction by Edward Lucie-Smith (Macmillan Caribbean) is published and launched at The Jonathan Clark Gallery, London, UK.

2004: 'My Jamaica' launches at Devon House, Kingston with an accompanying exhibition of paintings from the book.

2005: 'My Jamaica' launches at Books & Books, Coconut Grove, Miami, Florida, USA.

2005: Exhibition of new paintings at Dharma Studio in Coconut Grove, Miami, Florida, USA.

2006: Participates in a major group show comprising fifty artists from fifty countries entitled, 'What is Realism?' curated by Edward Lucie-Smith, Albemarle Gallery, London, UK.

2006: Group show at Dharma Studio, Coconut Grove, Miami, Florida, USA.

2007: Group show, 'The Enduring Landscape', Dharma Studio, Coconut Grove, Miami, Florida, USA.

2008: Presents 'An Evening with Edward Lucie-Smith: The Curator in conversation with Dr Jonathan Greenland' at Artist's studio, Montrose Rd, Kingston, Jamaica.

2010: Contributes to 'Art Jamaica' New Hall College, University of Cambridge, UK.

2011: 'My Jamaica' exhibition of new paintings and book launch at The Jonathan Clark Gallery, London, UK.

2013: Exhibition: 'My Jamaica: the Paintings of Judy Ann MacMillan', Spanish Court Hotel, Kingston, Jamaica.

2014: Auction and exhibition entitled, 'The Art of Resistance: defending academic freedom' presented by CARA (Council for Assisting Refugee Academics) in collaboration with New Hall College, University of Cambridge, UK.

November 2016: Exhibition 'Still Painting: after all these years' in association with Digicel and the Embassy of France, Kingston, Jamaica.

Awards:
Bronze Medal, Festival Exhibition, 1969
Caribbean Hall of Fame, 2007

Collections:
University of The West Indies
Bank of Jamaica
National Gallery of Jamaica
Aaron Matalon
Wallace Campbell
New Hall College, University of Cambridge, UK.

Acknowledgements

Sometimes things are best left unsaid but this is not one of those times. At this time, I would like to give thanks to my beloved family, especially my son Alexei, for your love and emotional support. Your faces have lifted my heart every time I have looked at you. You have been the great joy of my life.

To my dear friends I would like to say, thanks for sharing your lives with me. For the good times, the years of laughter, the lifelong conversations and also for the angst, the tears that brought us closer together.

To the collectors who bought my paintings, thank you for having faith in me. Your response kept my dream alive. I could not have done it without you.

Finally, special thanks to Nick Gillard who commissioned this autobiography many years ago. He planted the seed and he nurtured the manuscript with patience and sensitivity and through it all, he made me laugh. Nick predicted that my earlier book, *My Jamaica* would change my life and it did.

What will happen now?